THOUGHTS OF A
MILLWALL
OPTIMIST

THOUGHTS OF A
MILLWALL
OPTIMIST

FIVE YEARS IN THE LIFE
OF A MILLWALL FAN

DAVID HALL

AMBERLEY

First published 2010

Amberley Publishing
Cirencester Road, Chalford,
Stroud, Gloucestershire, GL6 8PE

www.amberleybooks.com

Copyright © David Hall 2010

The right of David Hall to be identified as the Author
of this work has been asserted in accordance with the
Copyrights, Designs and Patents Act 1988.

British Library Cataloguing in Publication Data.
A catalogue record for this book is available from the British Library.

ISBN 978-1-4456-0220-2

Typesetting and Origination by Amberley Publishing.
Printed in Great Britain.

CONTENTS

FOREWORD

When I decided to write this book, the idea was to put down in words how an ordinary fan felt about what was happening at his club, both the actual matches played and the day-to-day events that occurred during the season. I thought then that five years would be enough to get the flavour of what happened at a club like Millwall from a fans point of view, but I did not expect those five years to be as full of incident as they were, even by Millwall standards.

When year one brought enough changes in both chairman and manager to keep the proverbial revolving door busy, and resulted in relegation to League One, being the optimist that I am, I expected an immediate return to the Championship, not another relegation battle.

It was then that I thought that it would be poetic if promotion occurred in the final year of my five year plan, only to have that almost snatched away when the club reached the play-off final in year four.

As far as promotion then was concerned, even for an optimist like me, it was not going to happen as I hoped, especially as the fifth season started so badly.

But this is Millwall after all and they never cease to amaze. So here it is. How I felt about dropping down to bouncing back up, and all the blips and dips that occurred in between.

You might not agree with all or any of these thoughts but you must agree they make interesting reading, and a great insight to a club like this.

ACKNOWLEDGEMENTS

First of all thanks to Gary Alexander for missing his hat-trick goal at Wembley in the play-off final of 2009 and to Paul Robinson for scoring his winning goal at the same end in the corresponding match, at the same venue, one year later. Without both of you, the symmetry that this book has would not have been possible.

Thanks to Brian Tonks and Chris Bethell for the supply of pictures that give the book something to hang the words on.

Thank you Millwall Football Club. Without you I would never have known the joys and exasperations that watching football could bring.

A big thank you to Joe Pettican at Amberley Publishing, whose editing and ideas gave the book the shape you find it in today.

Finally and most importantly, thanks to all my family and friends who sit with me in the Lower East Stand (you all know who you are), for making my Millwall experience as good as it is. It just would not be the same without you all there.

CHAPTER ONE

ALL CHANGE
SEASON 2005/2006

CLOSED SEASON

It certainly is a strange closed season. Ever since Jeff Burnige took over as chairman, I have been trying to think who will be our new manager now that Dennis Wise has gone, and although I've thought of many possibilites, we're still waiting for an announcement and the start of a new season is getting nearer.

The players that have left have been a bit of a shock. Not that they have gone but the number of them, and all before a new manager has been appointed. Darren Ward I expected to go but not to Crystal Palace. I thought he could do better than that and go to a Premiership club. I thought maybe Wigan, who could do with a class defender now they have been promoted or, dare I say it, West Ham, but Palace, he could at least have moved out of the Championship.

Paul Ifill, well I expected him to go as well but I wonder how long it will be before Sheffield United has him on the injured list. The club will miss his trickery I suppose but he was not playing much last season so we won't miss him too much and as for Wise, well I hope Harry Redknapp is looking over his shoulder at Southampton, because who knows what will happen there if Wise decides to go back into management.

I can't see why we are waiting to make the announcement about a new manager for so long. Jeff Burnige is hopefully trying to get it right but the rumours about whom it will be are a little worrying.

It is strange when you look back though, and now that George Burley has come on the scene, then maybe holding out wasn't so bad after all, although what would have happened if Burley had stayed with Derby who knows. Maybe we would have had somebody named by now. Of course all this has had an unsettling effect on the players and indeed the fans. Seems we have not sold as many season tickets this year as the whole of the family enclosure last year so I suppose that says something.

* * *

I am not surprised that Burley turned the job down but the surprise was the appointment of Steve Claridge. Not that I don't think he will be a good manager and he will certainly get the approval of the fans as he is such a favourite here but that it all happened so quickly. Still, taking the squad off to an army boot camp might get their minds on getting fit for the start of the season and not on the loss of players. I expect Claridge will start to get some new players in soon.

Talking of surprises, Dave Tuttle was a shock choice as assistant manager but maybe he has done a good job behind the scenes that we do not know about. Now all we need is a decent coach. Maybe Steve Gritt will get his old job back.

Typical of Peter Sweeney not to turn up for the first day of training without letting anyone know, he has gone to Stoke. Well maybe they will find out he is not as good as he thinks he is and like Ifill he'll probably spend more time on the treatment table than the pitch.

Just what is going on? Dichio and Lawrence up for sale as well and although we need to save on the wage bill the break-up of the squad looks bad. Too many fans, including members of my own family, are already talking about relegation and although I think we are better than that, I can understand their fears. However, the young players have enough about them to finish around mid table and if Claridge can get a few old heads in then that will help as well.

* * *

How many more shocks can a fan take in just a few months? Burnige resigns and Dichio is off to Preston. At least Lawrence is staying but now Theo Paphitis is back in charge as chairman, if only for a short time, maybe things will stabilise.

It will seem strange not going to any pre-season matches. I don't think I have ever gone a season without seeing at least one but I'm off on holiday

Theo Paphitis (left) returns to The Den. (*Brian Tonks*)

to Scotland so I will just have to keep in touch with what is going on long distance and if we get back in time I might still go to the Iran game.

* * *

Okay, the friendly matches are not going well but we still need a few new faces. I don't know a lot about Sammy Igoe but Claridge seems to have faith in his ability and they played together so hopefully he knows enough about him. Not sure Don Hutchinson is the answer but John Oster might be a good bet and he will probably get us a few goals. They might be playing on trial in these friendly games, and the results are not going our way but at least we can give it time. The Iran match has been cancelled, I thought it would be after all the bombing that has been going on, don't want the club blamed for any trouble that some idiots might cause at the game.

So I guess the first match I'll see is the away game at Leeds, even if it is only on the television. I do agree with the supporter's club about the police there and we should not be held to ransom about travel and tickets but I wanted to go, not just because it is the first game of the season but it was somewhere new for my daughters Danielle and Eloise to go, we could not get there last season.

* * *

Thirty-six days in, I don't believe I'm reading this. Claridge has gone without a single league match having been played and Colin Lee has taken over as manager, and to think he was only there to be interviewed for the role of

Colin Lee takes over as manager.
(*Brian Tonks*)

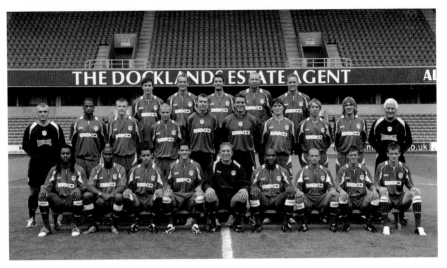

Team for the start of the 2005/2006 season with Colin Lee (centre front) now as manager. (*Brian Tonks*)

coach. Just goes to show that you can never be sure of anything in football and the season's only a few days away. Now the doom and gloom merchants will really have the bit between their teeth.

So we let John Oster go and sign Don Hutchinson. Oh well, we'll see. I seem to remember Jamie Vincent at Derby, not a bad left back as I recall, so maybe he can teach young Tony Craig a thing or two in the six months he's here. I don't know a thing about Carlos Fangueiro so we will have to wait and see when his international clearance comes through.

Well here goes. The season starts here.

AUGUST

7 August 2005, Leeds United 2 – 1 Millwall

Well not as bad a start as everyone said it would be. We did not get smashed, in fact it was a lucky bounce that gave Leeds their first and the penalty was one of those things. Didn't Hutchinson take his goal well? We deserved at least a draw but maybe all the sceptics will start to change their minds soon. Not sure about the 4-5-1 formation but away from home and against Leeds, maybe it wasn't a bad idea. Hopefully they will play a different formation on Tuesday or at least the same as the second half today.

David Livermore wants to leave now and although he is injured at the moment that will be another big blow. Hope he changes his mind. Still none of the players that left us in the summer have started for their new clubs, except Ifill who looks like he had a great game. That is a bonus and a better one is that Palace lost at home to Luton.

* * *

9 August 2005, Millwall 0 – 0 Coventry City

Adrian Serioux has got to learn not to get wound up so easily. We might have won if he had stayed on the pitch but ten men for almost all the second half and so quickly after the first game, no wonder the team looked tired. Marvin Elliott in particular looked shattered, but having just come back from having mumps, what should you expect? Still 0-0 against Coventry wasn't bad in the end and although they got away with murder, we stuck at it. At least the fans were surprised at how well we played and that must cheer them up a bit, and Bob Peeters gave us a laugh, as usual, when he came on. Surely we can't stick to this defensive formation for much longer. Changing it when we are forced to is not the answer. Fangueiro looks good, although he is obviously short of fitness.

Palace lost again and go bottom of the division, which must cheer a few people up as well. Bet Jordan wishes he had not guaranteed them promotion.

* * *

13 August 2005, Millwall 0 – 1 Stoke City

Maybe three games in seven days was a bit too much. Stoke took their goal well but the game as a whole was a bit boring and it lost its way. The referee didn't help, as usual, and we must start to play with two strikers or the opposition defence has nothing to do. Now we're bottom of the table so I'm not laughing now, still it's only goal difference that is the reason we are there.

Livermore played for the first time this season and the 'boo boys' were at him straightaway. Shouldn't we be cheering him on, rather than booing him if we want him to stay? I can understand why he wants to leave but that sort of behaviour from the fans won't encourage him to stay.

Don't expect to get much from Reading next Saturday so we'll probably still be bottom next week as well. At least Bob Peeters has gone. I hope he gives FC Genk as good a laugh as he gave us. Still I'm not sure about the Belgium sense of humour.

It looks like Livermore's move to Southampton is off. Did they think we would give him away? At least we don't have any qualms about playing him and we need his experience in midfield.

* * *

20 August 2005, Reading 5 – 0 Millwall

Well we need a goalkeeper now and quickly. Maybe 5-0 against Reading wasn't a true reflection of the game, especially as we lost Lawrence after fifteen minutes and Hayles soon after, and with Marshall sent off in between them it was always going to be a struggle. I thought we might be in with a chance of a point when I heard the team, playing two up front, but how quickly things can go wrong.

Maybe it's a freak result but the players are as low as the fans now and with no goalkeeper in the club with Masterson injured as well, we have a problem.

Just what will happen in the Carling Cup on Tuesday? Bristol Rovers will be looking to capitalise on our problems and who can blame them. Still it will be good to see Robbie Ryan again.

* * *

23 August 2005, English League Cup, Millwall 2 – 0 Bristol Rovers
Not sure what would have happened if Adrian Serioux had played in goal against the Pirates but the signing of Paul Jones was a good one even if it is only for a month. I hope he stays longer though as he made a couple of good saves and he certainly helped in organising the defence, which did look a bit shaky at times, having said that it was nice to get a win. Hayles' goal was all down to Ben May not giving up, and Fangueiro's reminded me a bit of Tim Cahill, getting up in the air like that. Maybe this will give them the confidence they need for the game against Ipswich on Saturday.

I will reserve judgement on the signing of Carl Asaba until I have seen him a few times. I'm not too sure about him from when I've seen him play against us but I suppose that could be for all sorts of reasons.

* * *

27 August 2005, Millwall 1 – 2 Ipswich Town
Well he did not play too badly I suppose but I bet Colin Lee wishes he had kept Jones in goal. Marshall was awful. It was his fault for the first goal and he remained dodgy throughout the game. He could have done better with Ipswich's second. What a goal by Ben May though. Don't suppose there will be a better one scored all season. He should have started the match.

Even with Richard Naylor being sent off, the referee made some very poor decisions against us and even though I don't think we are playing that badly we are still bottom of the table, still looking for that first win.

* * *

29 August 2005, Luton Town 2 – 1 Millwall
So Carl Asaba is injured already. Have we bought another nag? The game against Luton just about summed things up for us; go behind, fight back, get a goal and then lose. Another poor referee. Ben's goal should have at least given us a point. So we end the month with only one point. Still with a week's break we can regroup and the transfer window closes on Wednesday so I wonder whom we will get in.

* * *

Nobody, not a single new face, lots of rumours but no new players. At least we can still get loans from next week but that does not help now does it. John Sutton went to St Mirren without us seeing anything of him really. Wonder why? Oh well things can only get better. I am beginning to wish George Burley had taken the job now, he has taken Hearts to the top of the Scottish Premier League but I still have faith in the side and what Colin Lee is trying to get them to do.

SEPTEMBER

That was not very nice of Southampton to say that Dave Livermore has a dodgy knee. They must have been trying to get him on the cheap. Still we have got him still and all the better for it I say. Hope he stays now and doesn't go out on loan or move on next January.

We could still do with a couple of new faces, heard lots of talk but nothing concrete. Still I reckon that a win against Preston, then maybe pinching a point from Wolves, and then beating Sheffield Wednesday will get us climbing the table, although nobody seems to believe me.

David Tuttle as assistant manager – could do a lot worse. He has put a lot into the club since he has been here so I hope it works well for him. I don't know much about Stephen Constantine as a coach, although I have seen his CV and it doesn't look too bad, and now that the FA have finally lost out on that ridiculous racist charge we can start to move on. Bring on North End.

* * *

10 September 2005, Millwall 1 – 2 Preston North End

All right, it didn't go to plan. Our luck is certainly out. I thought Hutchinson's equaliser had won a point for us but we seem doomed to have bad luck on our side at the moment. Yes Elliott didn't play all that well but at other times the ball would have gone safe after that tackle, not to an opposing player who then goes on to score the winner.

I do not think Colin Lee was right to say the players lacked talent. Maybe he is trying to build them up a bit but it could work against him there.

Three new players have arrived in two days. See, I said things would be looking up. Don't know much about Ady Williams, although I think I remember him from Reading and I've seen Phillip Ifil on the television. Jermaine Wright though – we should never have let him leave here when he was a kid, and all three playing against Wolves, might get that point now.

* * *

13 September 2005, Wolverhampton Wanderers 1 – 2 Millwall
Three points and only ninety-nine Millwall fans saw it. What a debut for all of them but for Wright to score as well was just terrific. Hayles needed that one to give him some confidence as well. Colin Lee will have a few problems soon in picking a side, especially when Lawrence, Elliott and Asaba are fit again. We'll be off the bottom come Saturday night.

* * *

17 September 2005, Sheffield Wednesday 1 – 2 Millwall
I told you disbelievers. Hayles again, and Asaba scores his first for the club. Shame it was at Ben May's expense and hopefully the injury to his back won't be too bad but we are off the bottom now. It will be nice to get that first league win at home but first let's keep on winning by beating Yeovil on Tuesday.

* * *

20 September 2005, English League Cup, Yeovil Town 1 – 2 Millwall
Okay, so Yeovil had a player sent off but it was after Dunne and Hayles had scored and we weathered the storm after they scored as well, so it shows we can do it without the loan players playing. Don't know where all that extra time came from at the end but who cares, we're through. Hope we get a big team now and start another cup run.

Mansfield! We drew Mansfield away! Still I suppose it gives us a chance to get through to the next round as well. Maybe we'll get a big club next, or maybe it will help get us through to the final, who knows.

Wonder what will happen after Saturday, Jones' loan ends then. He has only played the once so I am not sure if he will want to stay even if we can afford him.

* * *

24 September 2005, Millwall 0 – 0 Cardiff City
FIFA World Fair Play Day, who is kidding whom? No referee ever seems to play fair where Millwall are concerned and certainly not Andy D'Urso. He should have sent off Cardiff's Weston and the way he treated Morris was nothing like fair. Sending him off with just seconds to go was unbelievable. Mind you I was surprised to hear that was his first suspension of his career.

Still, I suppose a 0-0 draw was just about right and it was good to see Lawrence back, even if it was because Phillips was injured again. At least Jones is staying for another month. I do not know what will happen if Marshall gets injured when he has gone, as we don't have any cover at all at the moment.

* * *

27 September 2005, Millwall 1 – 1 Queens Park Rangers
The news about Adrian Serioux going back to Canada was a shame. Still I suppose his mother being ill and being such a long way from home would play on his mind. Hope things sort themselves out soon and we see him back here in the not too distant future.

Good to see Hayles scoring regularly again but we should have beaten QPR. I suppose a point is better than nothing, but Bircham was up to his old tricks again, and we really should have won the game. Still it could have been worse I suppose, the 'Lion Tattoo Man' or Stefan Moore could have provided us with one of those 'Against our old club' moments. When will we get our first home win of the season?

* * *

30 September 2005, Hull City 1 – 1 Millwall
Another 1-1 draw! Should have beaten Hull, and we would have done if Wright had put the late chance away. Still, we're out of the relegation zone at the end of the month and that is a good sign.

Hope the club investigate what happened with the coach that the Humberside police turned back to London. Don't know the whys or wherefores but they were Millwall Supporters Club members and they had tickets, and to think it was the police who changed the match to a Friday night in the first place.

OCTOBER

First day of October and we're back in the relegation zone again. Could be worse I suppose, we are not bottom, but that is what happens when you play on a Friday night.

Still there are no games for a couple of weeks now because of the World Cup qualifying games, so I am off on holiday.

* * *

15 October 2005, Norwich City 1 – 1 Millwall
I come back to the news that Sammy Igoe wants to leave. Well not to leave exactly but to go on loan to help keep him match fit. I think he's not a bad player but Colin Lee obviously doesn't rate him much. I suppose Igoe is thinking about what will happen when the loan players go back to their own clubs at the end of the year. I did wonder about that myself.

I suppose I'd have taken a draw before the game at Norwich, especially with both Lawrence and Phillips out through injury again but I wished it had been three.

Good to see Williams get his first goal for the club but Marshall does seem to have a nightmare when he plays against his old clubs. He was definitely at fault for the Norwich equaliser. Still he redeemed himself when he saved Huckerby's penalty.

Huckerby does seem to go down at the slightest touch, yet I don't remember him doing that when he played for us on loan early in his career. Maybe that's what playing at a higher level teaches you. Why though did Hayles have to complain so much? Second booking and off he goes. Now he will miss the game against Sheffield United, having said that he does moan too often for my liking. If he put as much effort into playing as he does to moaning and falling over, he might score more often.

However, we are not a dirty side but six bookings in this game and a sending off – that's the third so far this season – and not a vicious tackle made in any game so far. It's our reputation again I suppose.

I am glad Colin Lee feels the same as me, and I suspect most fans do too, when he says we are being victimised by referees and has had the guts to say so in print. I expect the authorities will censure him for that but somebody had to say it. He's given the coaching job to Constantine until the end of the season as well. Maybe that will help.

* * *

18 October 2005, Millwall 0 – 4 Sheffield United

Thought we were the better side for the first twenty minutes tonight and if we had a goal scorer we might have been three up before Sheffield United scored. When they did, our heads seemed to drop and to be honest there was probably no way back then. We were not four goals worse than them though and I was a bit disgusted with how they kept falling to the floor at every opportunity, especially Pericard.

Ben May did his best on his own up front but he needed help. Still as I said already, Dunne and Phillip Ifil could have put us in front and then, who knows? Still I think Sheffield will win the division. They really did look good.

Not sure what Paul Ifill expected. He must have known he would get booed all the time, and he didn't get a sniff all night. Wherever he went, Vincent, Ifil and Lawrence had him in their pocket. He could have acknowledged us when he was substituted though. We clapped him off, why did he ignore us? Wonder what sort of reception Wise will get on Saturday?

Good to hear the club have done something about the fans that had trouble at Hull. At least they'll get their money back. Another lesson learnt for somebody I suppose.

* * *

22 October 2005, Millwall 0 – 2 Southampton

Why did Wise get clapped in the warm up and when he came on as a substitute? Worse still there were a few who sang that stupid 'Oh Wisey' song. Don't they realise he is the reason we are in such trouble at the moment?

Will we ever get this first home win though? We were never two goals worse than Southampton and if we had ten men we would have at least drawn the game. To think I thought Sheffield United went to ground easily, this lot were far worse. Must be the red stripes they wear.

Luck certainly goes against you when you are at the bottom. That was a terrible back pass from Vincent for the first goal and he could not move because of a hamstring problem he had and played them onside for the second. Furthermore, Ifil should never have been sent off. I know Higginbotham told the referee he had not touched him but in that case why did he collapse the way he did? Red card number four and we still have not made a bad tackle.

It could be worse I suppose. If George Burley had come here instead of Hearts maybe he would have walked out on us today instead of them, especially in the position we're in. Who would have thought it? And the club unbeaten at the top of the table; just goes to show that strange things really do happen in football. Let's hope the team pick themselves up for the Mansfield game. A good win there and then at Plymouth, could get us going.

* * *

25 October 2005, English League Cup, Mansfield Town 2 – 3 Millwall

We do live dangerously. Two up from May and Robinson, and looking like we are coasting it, then let them get back to equalise. Livermore's winner came right on time, quite literally. No way back then and what a goal for the winner. That'll stop the boo boys for a little while. Glad he wants to stay with us but if they don't get off his back then who can blame him if he goes in January. Wonder who we'll get in the next round?

Well at least it is a home match, but Birmingham. Hope there is no repeat of the trouble the last time we played them. Expect that will be an all member's game. Could have been worse I suppose, we nearly got Palace and those thieving scumbags are already charging us £30 to watch a league game there.

* * *

30 October 2005, Plymouth Argyle 0 – 0 Millwall

A point against Plymouth was better than nothing I suppose but we still can't score goals and we had the chances. We really need to take all three at Burnley on Tuesday and then get that first home win against Crewe. It's looking like a long hard week.

Still we've managed to keep Paul Jones here for another month. Don't know why though. Not that he is not a good goalkeeper but because we don't play him and we should. He's obviously costing us a bit of money and with Masterson back to fitness maybe he can gain some experience by being on the bench.

NOVEMBER

1 November 2005, Burnley 2 – 1 Millwall

Has somebody somewhere got it in for us? 0-1 up against Burnley after just 90 seconds with Wright's goal and then we lose 2-1, having three players sent off. The referee certainly lost us the game there. May sent off in the tunnel at half time, and then Morris, okay O'Conner was sent off with him but still, and then Marshall at the end for something he said. Good job we kept Jones now, as he'll be needed for Saturday.

Racist! Saying Ben May made a racist comment to Frank Sinclair. How could the referee send May off for that when even Sinclair said he didn't make such a remark, and then showing red to Marshall for telling him he had a nightmare of a game? Somebody should look into this and we should appeal.

Now we're told we can't appeal as there is no video evidence. How can you have video evidence for something that happened in the tunnel and anyway what good would that be for something that was said. Even worse, nobody else heard it, not even the other officials it seems. Just what is going on? We are in trouble now if our only fit and experienced strikers are Hayles and Braniff.

So Ben is thinking about taking Mr Beeby to court to get his name cleared. Good! Hopefully both he and the club will have the nerve to go through with it. It might make referee's start to think about the consequences of their actions. Just realised he was the same referee who sent off the Barnet goalkeeper at Old Trafford in the Carling Cup after just 45 seconds. Red must be his favourite colour.

Bruce Dyer! We've got Bruce Dyer in on loan. Hope we haven't brought in another inadequate player. Well he has scored goals in the past but with our record of bringing players like that to the club, I don't hold out much hope. Still, I could be wrong and if he does the business on Saturday I'll take it all back.

* * *

5 November 2005, Millwall 1 – 3 Crewe Alexandra

I was right, he is an ineffective player. Yes he won us the penalty that Hayles scored but he could have had a hat-trick to himself and then we hit the bar twice as well. I thought that was relegation for sure having lost 3-1 to Crewe, especially with them being the team above us but other results have gone in our favour so four from bottom is still only five points away.

Even more galling than losing is finding out that James O'Connor, sent off with Morris at Burnley, has had his red card rescinded.

The crowd abuse at Theo Paphitis was not called for. I know the fans were upset but how quickly they have forgotten that without him we probably would not be here and we have had some great times with him as chairman too.

Well it is an international break now and then off to play Sheffield United in a fortnight, and we'll probably beat them.

* * *

Good to see that Steve Cotterill and Frank Sinclair have been true to their word and backed Ben May over that racist slur. Hope he has the bottle to carry it through now and go to court to clear his name.

Marcus Stewart! Okay we might need some new players when those on loan go back but why do we seem to go for older players, often has-beens in my opinion. Why don't we try for some young wannabe instead?

* * *

Now Stewart says he wants to see how things go at Bristol City before deciding if he wants to come here. That does not sound good to me. If he only wants to come here because he cannot get into the Bristol side then why do we want him? We need players who want to come here, not those who come here because there is nowhere else.

* * *

19 November 2005, Sheffield United 2 – 2 Millwall

Okay, I take it back about Bruce Dyer. Well no, I will suspend judgement for a match or two. Still, his two goals against Sheffield United earned us a point and nobody gave us a chance of that. So what if they did hit the woodwork a few times, it is about time we got a bit of luck. Our new 3-5-2 formation certainly worked and it was good to see Ady Williams back from injury. Roll on Tuesday and maybe our first home win in the league.

* * *

22 November 2005, Millwall 1 – 0 Norwich City

What a day Tuesday was. First the rumours about Peter De Savary (or P. De S. as I have since found out he likes to be called) taking over as chairman of the club, then the announcement just before the game that he will take over from next Tuesday and then our first home league win. Such a lot to take in during one day, still that is what being a Millwall fan is all about I suppose.

I am still reserving judgement about Dyer but glad to see Marvin score the goal that sunk Norwich for that win. He looked delighted and I was for him. He's certainly getting back to the Marvin of old.

What a battling performance it was, especially with the team we put out. Only two recognised defenders in the side, yet along with Marvin, Livers had a great game in the centre of defence (we really must do all we can to keep him) and Dunne had Huckerby in his pocket all through the match. He didn't even win when diving, although he tried a few, especially in the penalty area.

Well we sent Jones home with a win and who knows maybe we can get him back again when the transfer window opens in January.

Doesn't look good for Saturday; Livermore is suspended; Williams and Marshall are injured again; Lawrence is already out; Wright is unable to play against his own club while on loan; and Masterson has chosen to go back to Ireland and quit football. We have only one central defender and no goalkeeper available. What will we do?

* * *

26 November 2005, Millwall 0 – 1 Leeds United

Well Colin Doyle solves the goalkeeping crisis, well at least for one match but he can't play against his own club, Birmingham, next Tuesday and Zak Whitbread solves the central defence problem, although he's cup tied as he has already played for Liverpool. Oh well it never rains but pours as they say. At least the rule that a player can't play against his parent club will stop Don Hutchinson scoring against us now he's gone to Coventry on loan.

Disgraceful! That's the only word I can use to describe how I feel about the Leeds fans that chanted anti-Manchester United stuff during the minutes silence for George Best's death. I had hoped it would not happen but had expected it too. Leeds manager Kevin Blackwell said it was a minority of fans that behaved that way and it might have been a minority if you take into account their home attendances but they were at The Den and it sounded like most of them to me.

Heartbreaking! That's the only word I can use to describe how I felt, and I'm sure that goes for the players and the rest of the fans, having lost due to an own goal in the third minute of time added on at the end. Ben May's deflection left Doyle with no chance and when you consider the team was changed yet again they put on a great performance. Not the way Paul Robinson would like to remember his first game as captain of the side I'm sure.

Doyle and Whitbread look good acquisitions, it is a shame they might not be with us long and as neither of them can play next Tuesday it is a good thing Livermore, Wright and Morris will be available again but with Dyer being cup tied and Hayles getting booked, which means he will miss the Palace and Coventry games, this team will never get a chance to play as the same unit twice in a row.

* * *

29 November 2005, English League Cup, Millwall 2 – 2 Birmingham City (Birmingham won on penalties)

What a night Tuesday was – first of all, an inspirational talk from P. De S., then the debut of Lenny Pidgeley, and then an incredible game against Birmingham. I do not know how I survived all that.

Shame Pidgeley was not here long enough to get to know the rest of the defence and Chelsea have a good goalkeeper in the making there but what a game. Behind twice and great goals from Dunne and Elliott, pity we could not win the penalty shoot out. Still I don't blame either Hayles or May for missing, although Hayles should have hit the target. Another set of changes in the side but that's been the nature of our season so far, so onto Selhurst.

DECEMBER

3 December 2005, Crystal Palace 1 – 1 Millwall

Oh no, not again. How many times are we going to lose points to last minute goals? I thought we could hold out after May's header and if Dyer's had gone in instead of hitting the bar then it was all over but for Palace to score in the ninety-third minute was too much to take. Last game for Ady Williams as well. Hope we can get him back in January. More changes to the side as well and there will be more next week at Coventry, and again for the match against Reading. I'll be glad when things settle down.

A home tie against Everton in the FA Cup should bring in the crowd. It will be good to see Tim Cahill again and I hope he gets a good reception but also that he goes away with his tail between his legs.

Now we are in trouble with Hayles needing an operation on his knee. Looks like he might be out for the rest of the season so who knows what might happen now. Still we've added a director to the board, Constantine Gontcas. Hope he also brings some money with him, especially as he works for an investment bank. This could be the start of something for us at last.

* * *

10 December 2005, Coventry City 1 – 0 Millwall

Another lost game and another red card. Losing 1-0 at Coventry was bad enough but we might have got something out of the game if Lawrence had stayed on the pitch. Are referees picking on us or something? Still young Marvin Williams looked promising when he came on. Now though, Wright and Ifil have gone back to their clubs and with nobody to replace them a long struggle over the Christmas and New Year period looms large.

* * *

17 December 2005, Millwall 0 – 2 Reading

It could have been so different if Dunne's header had gone in instead of hitting the bar and then Reading scored twice. Then adding insult to injury we have Tony Craig sent off as well. What's that saying about pouring rain? It certainly is at The Den at the moment and we need a goalkeeper again as Doyle's loan is up.

* * *

David Tuttle (left), Dennis Wise and Jeff Burnige look on glum faced. (*Brian Tonks*)

Wow! Another new manager, Dave Tuttle takes over in a caretaker role with Tony Burns as his assistant and Colin Lee becomes Director of Football. Whatever next? Roy Keane at The Den? P. De S. said he tried to get him and even if it is not true it shows the way he wants to go.

A bit of good news at last, David Livermore signs a new four and a half year contract and Doyle signs again, although on an emergency contract. Maybe Hayles' knee is not as bad as first thought either, the news gets better all the time. Hope the results start to follow. Still, with the army in to build our fitness at least we won't be too tired after the next run of games.

Dennis Wise walks out of Southampton because George Burley got the job and not him. Please don't let the rumours be right and he comes back here.

* * *

26 December 2005, Leicester City 1 – 1 Millwall

So nearly gave Tuttle a first game win. Okay, it was an own goal that gave us the lead and I suppose I would have taken a draw before the game so 1-1 is not the end of the world but having Robinson sent off as well! This is just getting silly. Glad we are appealing against this one.

* * *

28 December 2005, Millwall 0 – 0 Watford
A 0-0 draw against Watford but again the woodwork stopped us. If only Dyer's header had gone in but we're still unbeaten under Tuttle, now is the time for that first win.

* * *

31 December 2005, Brighton and Hove Albion 1 – 2 Millwall
Got it and off the bottom of the table at the end of the year and we came from behind to win. What a great idea of Tuttle to change three players at half time. Brighton didn't know what hit them and the goals from May and Simpson were great to see. Let's hope we can carry on like this in the New Year.

JANUARY

2 January 2006, Millwall 2 – 1 Derby County
So now we have a new phrase at The Den, 'You've been Marvined.' Again we were behind but Simpson and Williams certainly changed things when they came on. It was a great header by Elliott and young Williams' winner was straight out of dreamland. Now for Everton in the cup – I hope Marshall will be fit because Birmingham won't let Doyle play.

* * *

7 January 2006, English FA Cup, Millwall 1 – 1 Everton
Good to see Cahill clapped onto the pitch. Marshall certainly played his part to help us to that 1-1 draw. If only we could have held onto Williams' goal we would be playing Chelsea in the next round, still I suppose we can still do that after the replay. To think we did it without Dunne, Morris and Simpson. Hope that does not mean they were left out because they were being sold and we did not want to jeopardise that if they were cup-tied.

Vincent and Hutchinson have also come to the end of their contracts, so what will happen now? Just whom will we bring in and which of the many rumours will prove to be right? At least we've managed to re-sign Zak Whitbread until the end of the season and Bruce Dyer has thankfully returned to Stoke.

* * *

14 January 2006, Preston North End 2 – 0 Millwall
So Hutchinson has gone back to Coventry on loan until the end of the season. Thought he only had a six-month contract with us anyway so that's interesting. Lots of rumour about players coming in, especially a striker from Iceland. We

Tim Cahill returns to The Den for Everton in the FA Cup. (*Brian Tonks*)

could certainly do with a couple of strikers. At least we now have Colin Doyle on loan until the end of the season so that should help.

Well I did not expect us to get much at Preston. I had hoped we would get a point but losing 2-0 was maybe right. Not the best way to remember your first team debut but I suppose you have to start somewhere and Will Hendry will at least know he played a part no matter how small.

Hope the players did not have Wednesday night's replay at Goodison on their minds. Still at least we know why we had players missing in the first match. They all had injuries. Still I wish that Tuttle's 'caretaker' tag was removed, as I'm sure it is making it more difficult to sign players when they're not sure what's happening on the management front.

* * *

18 January 2006, English FA Cup, Everton 1 – 0 Millwall

It had to happen I suppose, only lost 1-0 to Everton and Cahill scores the goal. At least he did not celebrate scoring and he has earned my respect for that. Oh well, back to reality and fighting to get out of the drop zone. Bring on the Wolves.

Hutchinson's signed permanently for Coventry now and Dennis Wise has gone there too. Look out Micky Adams is all I can say about that. Sammy Igoe has gone to Bristol. Didn't do much while he was here but Phil Ifil is back. That is good and hopefully things will start moving forward.

* * *

21 January 2006, Millwall 0 – 0 Wolverhampton Wanderers
I can see why Wolves are the draw specialists in the division, but if we had a decent striker then it wouldn't have ended 0-0. We created so many chances to have scored a hatful and their goalkeeper made some good saves. Oh for a goal scorer!

* * *

We've got one. Never heard of Berry Powel but then I don't know much about Dutch football. £125,000 doesn't sound too bad either, especially if he can make the difference. Apparently he watched the Wolves match so he knows we can make chances. Let's hope he can put them away.

One in one out now Shaggy has put in a transfer request. Maybe it is just to show his displeasure about a lack of signings and he doesn't really want to leave, I hope not because we don't want to lose him.

Maybe it worked. No sooner had Lawrence complained about the lack of signings than we get another player in. Not sure I know a lot about Lloyd Dyer either and hopefully he isn't like the previous Dyer we had (who really was dire) but apparently he's a very fast winger and a free buy from West Bromwich Albion. Another piece in the jigsaw I hope and it looks like Tuttle now has the job at least until the end of the season. Good!

Well it never ceases to amaze me how things go at The Den. Now Colin Lee has resigned – or was he pushed. Either way he has gone.

* * *

31 January 2006, Cardiff 1 – 1 Millwall
What a way to start your Millwall career, an equalising goal after just three minutes on the pitch. The 1-1 draw at Cardiff was a great point so let's hope that Berry Powel can produce the goods.

FEBRUARY

Looks like Tony Craig is wanted as the club have offered him an extended contract. Hope he signs and it means that Jamie Vincent has now gone back to Derby for good. Look out Sheffield Wednesday we want the three points.

* * *

4 February 2006, Millwall 0 – 1 Sheffield Wednesday
Neither team played well but what a way to lose. The referee needs shooting or at least removed from the list. He certainly gave a goal from Craig's corner kick and the Wednesday players thought so as well, but to disallow it and then

let them take a free kick and score from it while we were still celebrating at the corner flag at the other end of the pitch was disgraceful. What a terrible way to lose.

It is not even worth appealing as nothing will come of it. It is another three points we have had taken from us.

Heard a rumour that John Gregory has been lined up to take over as manager, don't know when but it's worth keeping in mind at the end of the season.

I suppose the old boy network will work against us again on Saturday now that Gary Waddock is in charge at Queens Park Ranger and Paul Jones has signed for them as well. No doubt Marc Bircham will score the winner as well.

Now Jermaine Wright has gone to Southampton. Are we destined to be haunted this way until the end of the season?

* * *

11 February 2006, Queens Park Rangers 1 – 0 Millwall

Not a good game at QPR. We did not really have a shot on goal and the players looked as if they were ready for relegation. Dunne looked like he wanted to get sent off and he certainly made sure it happened with those tackles, although Bircham did not help much. We didn't defend well when they scored the goal either, so things are not looking good now.

It would be a laugh if it was not serious. First we hear that we are trying to sign Darren Byfield and then read that Kim Grant is training with the team and could be re-signed. Oh well, we will see what happens against Hull on Tuesday. We will probably have no one by then. Still at least we know why Powel was substituted on Saturday. I hope he gets better quickly although he seems to have been sick ever since we signed him. Hope he doesn't turn out to be another dud.

* * *

14 February 2006, Millwall 1 – 1 Hull City

Well I suppose one point is better than none but we should have done better than drawing 1-1 with Hull. Livermore scored a great equaliser and it is about time we scored the late goal and not the opposition. However, it still seems that everyone is conspiring against us as again, we had ten men for most of the game and I thought the clash was caused by Marshall not Robinson. What a way to wake up from concussion to be told you had been sent off. Anyway, we had more shots at goal than we have had for ages and played much better so let's hope we can keep it up.

Just seen that Joe Healy has gone on loan to Walton and Hersham, well we are saying the players lack experience, so let's hope this gives him some.

* * *

18 February 2006, Millwall 1 – 1 Crystal Palace

Another late goal, this time from May, and another 1-1 draw, serves Palace right as they did exactly the same to us at their place. However, we aren't making the chances now either and that's a worry. At least that diving cheat Morrison didn't score but what has Ben Watson got against us. We seem to be the only side he will score against. Mind you, their fans caused more problems, £10,000 worth to be precise with damage to the seats and the walkway. We should claim the money back from them.

Well the good news is that Grant went to AFC Wimbledon and that Hayles and Asaba are ready to start training. Not sure about Asaba but I suppose he could be useful in a tight spot.

The bad news is that Morris is probably out for the rest of the season with a broken cheekbone, which he did in training on Friday. So now we know why he didn't play against Palace.

There has been interesting news about P. De S. trying to build a casino and hotel around the ground in the hope of making some money for the club. If it works fine but if not, well who knows? I suppose some fans will say that is all he's here for and that the ground will be sold next but we will have to wait and see.

Just seen that Asaba is fit but surely not match fit, so I hope he doesn't play against Stoke tomorrow.

* * *

25 February 2006, Stoke City 2 – 1 Millwall

He did and we lost but it was another dodgy refereeing decision that gave them their equaliser. Even the Stoke fans were amazed to be awarded a penalty like that and I thought we could hold onto May's opening goal. Our heads dropped again and I suppose losing 2-1 was not as bad as it could have been. With the other results going our way again we are still in there with a fighting chance.

MARCH

If we survive relegation this season it looks like we might be in for more of the same next season as we have just had the announcement of a £2.4 million loss. I suppose that will mean the sale of more players and who else have we got that we will regret selling in a few years time? Moses Ashikodi is now playing at Glasgow Rangers and for the England under-21 team, and scoring. It seems like we should have kept him and not McCammon.

Some good news, Ray Wilkins will be doing some coaching at the club until the end of the season. That might help lift a few spirits and so will the arrival of Colin Cameron form Wolves. It might only be for a month but he will bring some life to the side as he's a busy player and maybe we can get him for the rest of the season too.

* * *

4 March 2006, Millwall 2 – 1 Luton Town

Another late goal and three points, what more could you ask for? Well not being brought that close to heartache I suppose but Williams took the goal well and May's opener was good too. Add to that the fact that we managed to survive the Uriah Rennie show and the others down at the bottom with us all losing except Crewe and Derby, who both drew, hope is growing.

Well that's another one signed up as Paul Robinson signs for another two years. Not sure what it means but there is life in the old team yet, I hope.

How surprising that the newspapers have not reported the fact that Luton fans smashed up the walkway to the train station and this straight after the damage caused by the Palace fans. If it had been us causing the damage it would be all over the papers and everyone would be calling for us to be banned again.

I suppose that is what happens when you support a club with a reputation like we have. When will somebody print the truth about Millwall these days and help the world to see what it's really like at The Den. If that ever happened maybe we would start getting treated properly by officials as well as the man in the street. Dream on.

* * *

11 March 2006, Ipswich 1 – 1 Millwall

I would have taken a point at Ipswich before the game so I suppose I must be happy with the 1-1 result. Great goal by Livermore right at the death, we'll be getting a reputation as late goal specialists soon but it shows that we won't give up.

Mind you we still got our customary stupid decision and this time it was Craig who got sent off. How could he get booked for time wasting when Tuttle took the ball from Whitbread and gave it to him to take the throw-in?

That is thirteen red cards so far this season (fourteen if you count the rescinded one on Robinson) and apart from Morris' retaliation at Burnley not a single bad foul among them. Maybe the authorities are getting their own back on us this way because we've beaten the false accusations that have been made against us.

All the other teams around us drew as well today so we haven't made up any ground but at least we haven't fallen behind again.

I thought that with Craig suspended Dyer would now get a run in the team but we've brought Jamie Vincent back until the end of the season, this time he's on loan from Yeovil and Dyer has left the club having his contract cancelled by mutual consent. Can't say I blame him really.

More good news with the fact that Barry Hayles is training again and played in a closed doors match against Chelsea. I suppose his experience will be an asset providing he puts as much effort into scoring goals as he does jumping around and complaining. I expect he'll have a part to play on Saturday.

It seems that Joe Healy's loan is doing him good and he is now staying at Walton and Hersham until the end of the season. I hope it gives us a good striker for next season and it seems like Barry Hayles might play a part in the game on Saturday. Well that might help even if it is only from the bench.

The training ground has been sold and then leased back. I know that's put £1.85 million into the club kitty but is this the start of something sinister? Will the stadium go the same way?

* * *

18 March 2006, Millwall 0 – 1 Leicester City

Well we played well and with a bit of luck could have scored. Hayles did come off the bench but it was to no avail as we lost 0-1 to Leicester. Even though Elliott hit the post it was the same old story, we can't put the ball in the net. With Sheffield Wednesday winning it will probably take a miracle to beat the drop but miracles do happen.

The new FIFA race abuse rule is interesting and it will be fascinating to see who they apply it to, and how and when. However, I bet that we are the first club in this country to have it used against them. Am I a cynic? Probably, but the odds are firmly stacked against us.

Goodbye to the MSC (Millwall Supporters Club) for next season and hello to the 1885 Club, same rules, different name. Will that and the fan on the board make any difference? Only time will tell.

* * *

So now we know what the redeveloping idea was all about. Build training facilities and hire them out for the Olympics and hopefully others where we can make money. That is all right if it happens that way and added to the new share issue which will bring in a guaranteed £4.22 million (and according to the board a hopeful £9.6 million) that should keep the club going for a while. It will be interesting to see what happens over the next few years. Spending £500 million on this redevelopment is quite a sum and we could have bought Manchester United if the money had been ploughed into the club instead.

Talking of United, it was interesting to hear that the idea to bring Roy Keane to the club as player-manager was real. Unrealistic perhaps but it was tried.

Transfer deadline day comes and goes with no new faces at The Den. They tried to get Gifton Noel-Williams from Burnley but apparently something went wrong and he went to Brighton instead. Guess we all know what that means. I hope at least we manage to extend Colin Cameron's loan until the end of the season and with Hayles and Asaba back, and Simpson on his way, it is like having three new faces, although I'm not sure about two of them.

* * *

25 March 2006, Watford 0 – 2 Millwall

Now it seems we might lose Simpson for next season as he might not get a work permit, having not played enough games this season. Yes he has been injured for a large amount of it but that's how it works. I hope the club want to keep him and try hard to do so.

Another game, another dodgy penalty awarded against us but this time it went our way as Marshall saved it and an inspired Asaba (at last) and May (why wasn't he on from the start?) scored to help us beat Watford 0-2. You would never have predicted that score before the game.

Shame Wednesday won as well but Southampton lost and maybe it is them we should look at to overhaul. Get more points than them and we definitely stay up. Now we really must take all three points from Brighton on Saturday.

Yippee! We managed to extend Cameron's loan until the end of the season. There is a twenty-four hour call back clause but thanks Mr Hoddle. It's a pity your team did not beat Sheffield Wednesday as well.

Oh no. David Tuttle has been nominated for the manager of the month award. Hope he does not get it or that's three points down the drain.

* * *

Well he didn't, Rob Kelly of Leicester got the award. They can say goodbye to three points on Saturday then. Shame they now look pretty safe.

It never rains but it pours down at Zampa Road at the moment. Now Berry Powel says he wants to go. I suppose I can't blame him if he's not even getting on the bench, however, I'd like to know why we bought him, Dyer and Fangueiro to the club if we aren't going to play them. Surely we look at them first and if you can't get on the bench before Braniff then things must be bad.

APRIL

1 April 2006, Millwall 0 – 2 Brighton and Hove Albion

It might have been April Fool's Day but just who were the fools? It was not the manager of the month award that lost us the game but the manager of the past. Mark McGhee put the right side out and although I said two goals in the first ten minutes would be enough to win the game I didn't mean them to come from the away side. Noel-Williams didn't score but he caused enough trouble and it looks like the spirit has totally gone from the players.

Leicester lost so that old curse still works. We might still be able to mathematically stay up but it looks doubtful now, even to an optimist like me.

Well we now have the fan on the board decision made. His name is Peter Garston and I hope he does well. He certainly seems to have some good ideas but like everything else we will just have to wait and see. Good luck Peter. However, there were only 1,155 votes cast between all five candidates so I suppose that says something about the apathy of the Millwall fans for this idea.

* * *

Here we go again and another change if the rumours are to be believed, Ray Wilkins to move from part-time coach to director of football. I really don't know what is happening anymore but this must have some sort of unsettling effect for both the players and the fans.

* * *

Now we have another board appointment with Simon Menneer being brought into the club to find ways of increasing the number of fans at each game. Seems he was head of Credit Suisse First Boston but just what will he do to increase the crowds.

Good and bad news always seems to come together with this club. First the good news – well to some anyway – is that Jody Morris is fit and will play at Derby. The bad news is that Wolves have recalled Colin Cameron. Tuttle says he is going to make changes for the game at Derby tomorrow so we'll have to wait and see.

* * *

8 April 2006, Derby County 1 – 0 Millwall

Yes there were changes except some things stayed the same in that we lost 1-0, had a clear cut penalty turned down, and lost Morris for the rest of the season with an injured knee after half an hour. Hayles didn't even play as his season is also finished with his knee injury reoccurring.

Sheffield Wednesday and Brighton losing helped a bit but Crewe won so we drop down a place and time is running out for the great escape to happen.

The 'Let 'em come back' society has been formed to try and get the fans back to matches. The idea of writing to various people on the club database that haven't renewed season tickets etc., sounds good and I hope it works, but I hope that doesn't mean we will be inviting back the hooligan element we strove so hard to get rid of.

Colin Doyle has said he would like to sign for us when his contract expires with Birmingham at the end of the season. Now that would be a good move and a first step to rebuilding the side and there have been rumours that Neil Ruddock wants to come to the club as manager although the *South London Press* report that the players want Tuttle to stay as manager permanently no matter what happens at the end of the season. Personally I'd just like things sorted.

Anyway here we are at Easter, with two games in three days; our fate could be sealed by Monday evening. We've got nothing to lose so why not go on all out attack? Now that would be something to see.

* * *

15 April 2006, Millwall 1 – 1 Plymouth Argyle

All out attack is no good if you can't put the ball in the net and although we did it three times, two were disallowed so the 1-1 draw with Plymouth has not helped at all, in fact we are now bottom of the table.

I'll give the benefit of the doubt that someone was offside when Powel 'scored', although he certainly wasn't, but Whitbread ran from the edge of the box to head his 'goal' and although the official reason was that the goalkeeper was blocked he was never going to get to the ball. I expected Williams' equaliser not to count as well but I suppose allowing us one goal justifies cancelling the others. Am I getting cynical or what?

Tuttle says he won't be manager next season so the search is now on. Watch this space as the rumours start.

* * *

17 April 2006, Southampton 2 – 0 Millwall

Well that is it; we are finally relegated, along with Brighton and Crewe. Losing 2-0 to Southampton brought our stay in this division to its end, at least for a while we attacked plenty but struggled to score, even though we did hit the bar. Mind you their first goal was never a penalty and they could not miss the second when we did not have a single player in our half in the final seconds of the game.

Dunne's season is over as he got a broken cheekbone in the match and it was also revealed that Livermore has been playing in pain for the last few games with a foot problem, so well done to him for winning the player of the year award. That is one in the eye for his detractors.

The new share issue has brought in around £5 million and with money probably coming into the club from clauses in the contracts of Ifill, Ward and Reid that could bring in around another £500,000. So let's see where this money goes.

Here is the next manager rumour. Ray Lewington is the favourite to take over next season. He was in the frame at the beginning of this one and never got the job so it would be an interesting appointment if he got it now. He certainly knows his way around the lower divisions so I suppose he would not be a bad choice.

Tuttle resigns and we get our fourth manager in one season. Okay, he is another caretaker and he has been here before so stand up Alan McLeary, who takes over for the last two games. I don't understand why Tuttle didn't stay on until the end but that's just another twist in the tail of this very strange and eventful season.

The season tickets for next year have gone up in price and I thought that they would have at least stayed the same. Mind you the various incentives that come with buying one might help but I'm not sure how much of a drop there will be in sales for next season now that we are relegated.

* * *

22 April 2006, Millwall 1 – 0 Burnley

I suppose I expected to see a lot of the youngsters in the side now that McLeary is in charge and there was nothing to play for. We got a win in our last home game. Williams took his goal well and the rest had pretty good games as well. Was quite impressed with Hendry and Pooley, both looked sound when they came on to make their debuts. I guess this is the future I see before me, well at least next season.

* * *

30 April 2006, Crewe Alexandra 4 – 2 Millwall

So we lost the final game at Crewe, although 4-2 really flattered them and a couple of their goals were a bit dodgy. May took his two goals well and I hope he stays for next season.

It was the same old story though. Powel needs to learn when to shoot and when to pass, and Phillips is not a right back although he is not a bad central defender. Elliott was a lot better with Hendry sitting just behind him so maybe that's the way to go.

* * *

So now the seasons over, hope we get a decent manager in for the next one and soon, so that we don't have the fiasco we had at the beginning of this one, and we get a few players to boost the squad. Maybe Doyle and Whitbread might come back and who knows maybe Ifil as well, although I doubt we'll get any of them.

Oh well, the promotion dreams starts again, although it won't be easy and I don't expect to get out of League One at the first attempt, even if it would be nice.

I wonder what will happen in the closed season.

CHAPTER TWO

DRAMATIC TURNAROUND SEASON 2006/2007

CLOSED SEASON

Well it didn't take long for McLeary to say he wanted the manager's job. I suppose that will be the cheap and easy option for De Savary to take. Some youngsters have signed back on, although none have first team experience but last season was not all bad as we got some money in for the sale of Reid, Ifill, Ward and Sweaney as clauses had been written into their contracts. It all helps I suppose.

What a day, a new chairman of the football club, Stewart Till, and a new executive deputy chairman (or should that be chairwoman?), Heather Rabbatts.

De Savary obviously could not take the heat from the fans so although he stays as chairman of Millwall Holdings (he has now shown his hand that he is there for the money to be made in the regeneration he has been talking about), Till takes over in the hot seat.

At least he knows about football and indeed the club as he has been both a season ticket holder and executive club member, and his business credentials are good so let us see what he is made of.

Rabbatts has been brought in mainly to sort out the regeneration side of things and help make the club some money. Like Till, she has a CBE after her name and her business credentials are good so let us hope we don't have to wait too long to see what she can do as well.

And just to think that this all took place on the day we signed a new player. All right Adam Cottrell is another youngster but he cost nothing and as Charlton does not want the young defender then why shouldn't we take him on. We'll probably need all the bodies we can get when the cull starts.

The Rampant Lion badge is back. Well not until next season and we don't know in what style but the club have agreed to the fans vote so maybe the club will start listening to some of the things the fans are saying. It's going to be an interesting few weeks before the season starts that's for sure.

There have been so many rumours about who the new manager will be, in fact who has even had an interview, that I am just giving up now and waiting until the final decision is made. However, I hope it is a good one.

* * *

Still no manager but another new signing, this time it is striker Gavin Grant from Gillingham. Strange really, because we could have had him at Christmas time last year when Richard Cadette recommended him to us while he was playing for him at Tooting and Mitcham. I am not sure why he did not come here then and went instead to Gillingham but he is here now and if he is as good as I have heard he is we could have a new star in the making.

* * *

Still no manager, this is getting boring, but we do have another director, Trevor Keyse, who has been a Millwall supporter for fifty years. He made his money in the timber business so I hope we don't attract a wooden manager, or players that play like dead wood.

Talking about dead wood, we have let go of all the players who have contracts running out, except for Jody Morris who is injured and probably won't play much next season anyway. That's eight players all together so goodbye Andy Marshall, Carl Asaba, Curtis Weston, Joe Healy, Sammy Igoe, Trevor Robinson, Josh Simpson and Carlos Fangueiro.

It will be interesting to see who replaces them and our main priority must be a goalkeeper as we now don't have one and Doyle won't be coming, as he's re-signed for Birmingham.

* * *

Place your bets on the new manager now. It seems as if it's between Ian Holloway and Nigel Spackman, and the winner is – Spackman. Let's hope he does well. He should have a few good contacts which should help, but isn't it strange that we seem to appoint managers who were once Sky Sports pundits – McGhee, Wilkins, and Claridge being the others. Let's hope he is another McGhee and not another Claridge.

It has been quiet for a while but now Nicky Milo has resigned from the youth academy, and I hope his replacement, Joe Little, will continue to bring the youngsters through to the first team. There is a total change of backroom staff on its way, Spackman has already asked Wilkins to stay and assist him.

He also says he has been working behind the scenes to get players in and that there are already three players who have said they would come. Apparently when their names are released they will be a big surprise, so come on Nigel surprise me.

* * *

Final game before relegation to League One, at Crewe, 30 April 2006. (*Brian Tonks*)

Well that was a surprise – or perhaps not, depending on your point of view. I thought we were trying to bring players into the club not let them go but Berry Powel has had his contract cancelled by mutual consent. That is £125,000 plus his wages wasted. I thought he would do well in League One, find his feet and score a few goals for us but it seems that our new manager did not rate him. We could have tried to sell him somewhere and recoup some of the money so I hope he doesn't come back and haunt us.

If you can't catch the Millwall bus try and catch the Millwall taxi. I am all for advertising the club and if this works then all I can say is well done to whoever thought it up.

Two out of three sign up in one day, both on three-year contracts and both for free. It looks like we're taking on the Gillingham strike force because after Grant comes Darren Byfield. A proven goal scorer at this level and remember he has already been the man of the match here when he scored four goals for Rotherham when they beat us 6-0 a few seasons ago. Followed by our first goalkeeper in, Lenny Pidgeley from Chelsea. I must say he impressed me in the game he played for us last season against Birmingham when he was here on loan for the week. Let's hope he is as good as he looked then.

If Zak Whitbread is the third signing then it is a good one and getting him back was quite a coup as I thought he would either stay at Liverpool or at least go to a Championship side, and a total payment of £200,000 depending on promotion and games played is good business as far as I'm concerned. He must really believe in us, we need to do the same. Promotion is already looking a possibility.

***

Now we have a new shirt sponsor and a new kit. The blue and white kit looks fine to me but I'm not sure about the black and plum change strip. I suppose I'll have to wait and see it for real, rather than photographs of it.

The new sponsor is a local estate agent called Oppida and apparently the name means 'unbreakable fortress', so let's hope The Den is like that this season and our defence is as often as possible.

It is not often somebody connected with Millwall that gets some recognition and although he has been gone from the club since 1977, I just want to put on record my congratulations to Gordon Jago for getting an MBE in the Queen's birthday honours for his services to global soccer. He was President of the World International Soccer League.

* * *

Now we have another new signing with the arrival of right-winger Filipe Morais from Chelsea. He has already played for Portugal's under-twenty side and as we got him for nothing that sounds good to me.

It is like waiting for a bus at The Den at the moment. Just as one new player signs then another one comes along. We have not had much joy in recent seasons in signing players from Scotland but hopefully left winger, Tom Brighton, will change all that. The people at Clyde, where we got him from and again for nothing, say he is the quickest player in the division. Well keep going Nigel as these are the kind of signings we have been waiting for and if they are successful then I see no reason why we can't get back into the Championship at the first attempt. Hope I have not put the *kybosh* on that now.

Nigel Spackman urges the players on.
(*Brian Tonks*)

Now maybe the final pieces of the behind the scenes staff have arrived as more backroom staff join the club with Willie Donachie coming in as assistant manager and Ade Mafe as the new fitness coach. Donachie has been around at some top clubs as a player and coach, so that sounds good and if Mafe can bring some of the Olympic medal winning skills to the team then the future looks bright.

Not too sure about Jody Morris signing for another year though. His injury will probably keep him out of the side for quite a long time but I suppose his experience will be welcome when we get to the sharp end of the season and it might be good to have him then. We'll just have to wait and see.

* * *

What a busy time at The Den over the last few days. Mark Phillips has re-signed and we have signed three more new players, midfield player Derek McInnes from Dundee United, goalkeeper Chris Day from Oldham and defender Richard Shaw from Coventry, and all of them were free.

Not too sure how the signing of Shaw will go down with the fans but according to Donachie he will be mainly a reserve player and coach, playing only if needed in the first team. However, I think he will play more often than he does not, so I hope he does well or the fans will hound him due to his connections with Palace. We'll just have to wait and see. Talking about Palace, Tony Burns has left and joined them.

Interestingly, he was in the squad that went on the two-match tour of Iceland but Kevin Braniff was not, so maybe that really is the end of him. Ben May was not with them either but that is because he needs an operation on his shoulder, which will keep him out for up to four months. Just when it looks like things had changed for the better. He might struggle to get in the side when he gets back to fitness if they are doing well.

* * *

Well we lost the first game in Iceland 2-0 and the second 4-0 but I suppose with so many new players it will take a while for them to gel and of course we have just come back to training while the opposition have been playing for some time and doing well so I'm not that concerned – well not at the moment.

Looks like Lawrence might be leaving as various clubs have shown an interest in him. I just hope he does not end up at Palace as well. Still at least we now have a goalkeeping coach to replace Burns. Kevin Dearden has been around a bit and has coached at Palace. I make that 1-1 at the moment then.

* * *

We have got some in, now we're about to lose some as well and this time it is David Livermore. I can't say I blame him as the way he was treated by some

Gordon Jago MBE – Millwall manager 1974-77 – with Barry Kitchener. *(Chris Bethell)*

of the fans has been diabolical. If I'd been booed like that I would have gone as well, this makes me wonder why Braniff still stays here. And now Hayles is talking to Plymouth and Elliott says he won't sign a new contract and wants to go as well. Here we go again!

Pat Holland is back at the club as chief scout. That has been left to run down since Tuttle became manager so let's hope we can rebuild the scouting network and really push on.

I suppose the FA fine for our disciplinary record last season could have been worse. They did suspend £40,000 of it but with a £20,000 fine suspended from last season and £10,000 paid, now it still sounds a lot. Let's hope we don't have that problem this season.

* * *

Three leave in one go, Hayles has gone to Plymouth, Livermore to Leeds and Paphitis has resigned from the board. I think that is a good move for Paphitis as it means that whatever the board do now, he can't be seen to have had any input.

I'm not happy about Berry Powel though. He's having a trial at Hibernian and they are thinking of signing him. We could have got a bit back for him if they wanted him. We really do like to throw money away sometimes.

Three home friendly matches before the season starts and we don't win any of them; 4-1 against Charlton, 1-0 against Reading and a 0-0 draw with

Palace. It does not look good on paper but they played well and with a bit of luck could and should have scored more. I sound a bit like last season there.

Anyway it does look good for the new season and we will see in a few days time. Wish the ticket office would get sorted out though. Just five days to go before the first game and they have only just sent out the season tickets. There will be almighty problems if some don't arrive in time for Saturday.

* * *

The season tickets arrived on Tuesday so that is a relief, especially as we have signed two more players. Don't know anything about Poul Hubertz but do know Neil Ardley well, he could be quite an asset to us as the season wears on and is very experienced. Hope they are both good signings.

* * *

Another day and another three players join the club. Don't know anything about any of them but I'm sure I will find out soon enough, so 'hello' to Chris Hackett, Samy-Oyame Mawene and Zoumana Bakayoko.

The squad numbers were released today but I am not sure what they indicate. If the numbers pick the first side to play, then barring injury, which is why Ben and Jody are not included, the side would be: Pidgeley, Craig, Elliott, Robinson, Whitbread, Dunne, McInnes, Byfield, Morais, and with Ben out injured and Lawrence just gone, I would guess that the other two would be Hubertz and Shaw and you can make any sort of guess about substitutes.

Of course that is also if the side play 4-4-2. If they play another system or other players arrive then who knows. Roll on Saturday.

Team for the start of the 2006/2007 season. (*Brian Tonks*)

***

Maurice Ross signed today making sixteen players in all so my selection has probably now gone out of the window. I can't wait for tomorrow. I am getting excited and that is not like me.

AUGUST

5 August 2006, Millwall 1 – 1 Yeovil Town
All right, a 1-1 draw was not the start we were hoping for but it could have been a defeat so that is the best way of looking at it.

Byfield took the goal well, although we were awful in the first half. Maybe that was a bit of stage fright and the fifteen-minute delay to get all the fans in could not have helped. Neither did the changes in formation and the fact that so many new players were starting together.

We must get a regular formation though and that means at least two strikers on from the start. The team all showed good touches and I'll reserve judgement until they have all had time to settle in.

***

8 August 2006, Leyton Orient 2 – 0 Millwall
Oh no! Last season is haunting me already, losing 2-0 at Leyton Orient. Craig sent off after only three minutes and Byfield carried off after twenty-five. Here we go again.

At least the club are going to appeal against Craig's red card. All the television replays showed he never touched the Orient player, but when did that stop referees from sending players off. This referee was the same one that sent off Paul Robinson last season, when he was being carried off on a stretcher, and that one was rescinded.

At least Byfield only has ankle ligament damage but he will still be out for quite a while and it could have been worse I suppose, he could have broken it. Isn't it typical Millwall?

More changes to the board as David Sullivan resigns. Well that is the Lewisham connection gone and that does not leave many from the old regime left.

***

Craig's red card was rescinded and he can play on Saturday, but it still remains against his name and the club's. That is not fair as far as I'm concerned. If it was wrong to give it why still keep it on record, especially with the disciplinary record we had last season.

Shame that Barry Cogan has gone to Barnet, I liked him but I suppose his chances would have been minimal with all the players we have that can play in that position. So Saltergate here we come and let's hope we take our first three points.

* * *

12 August 2006, Chesterfield 5 – 1 Millwall
Well at least our second away game this season was better than the one last season. Well we scored a goal didn't we, and Braniff took it well, maybe it will kick-start things for him, if he ever makes a starting position in the side. Shame it was just a consolation after Chesterfield had scored five. We really must get the defence sorted out though or things will get worse.

I know I don't normally get into the reserves but their first game of the season, even though it was a 0-0 draw, will have given Spackman a chance to see some of the other players in a match situation, so maybe we might see some changes against Oldham on Saturday.

I have heard a rumour that we are after another Scottish player, a defender from Glasgow Rangers called Bob Malcolm. Well I did say we needed the defence sorted out but will this be the right way? Well we have to sign him first I suppose.

* * *

The Bob Malcolm deal is off. The clubs both agreed terms but he would not agree personal terms. I do not know what they were but hope he wasn't asking for silly money. Anyway, Spackman will have to sort out the defence another way now.

* * *

19 August 2006, Millwall 1 – 0 Oldham Athletic
Alan McLeary left the club today. The backroom revolution is practically complete and Richard Shaw will now manage the reserve side. They do not have many games to play in a season anymore so that won't be too difficult.

Well the defence was certainly sorted with Whitbread going to left back – I think he is better there – and Robinson coming into the middle. Oldham were a stern test and we needed that win and although it was only by one goal, it got Hubertz off the mark and maybe he can get a place in the starting line up now. Must say Braniff had a good game in his first start as well. Never thought I would see the day when he got clapped off.

More rumours and this one is about us signing Nacho Novo from Rangers. He's a good striker I know but although we can afford the transfer fee I am not sure about the wages he will want and as Preston are supposed to be looking at him as well, that is where he'll go, you can guarantee that.

* * *

22 August 2006, English League Cup, Millwall 2 – 1 Gillingham

Two wins on the trot, now that is something. I thought we played well in larger patches than before so it is coming together slowly. Both Braniff and Hubertz took their goals well but it is a shame that we gave Gillingham a chance to score as well. A clean sheet would have been nice. The two French boys looked good on their first start so maybe we have a bit of strength in depth this season. Hope we get a big club in the next round. Maybe the Carling Cup will be good for us.

So, Will Hendry has had his contract cancelled. I liked the look of him when he played at the end of last season but again I suppose with so many players coming in things like this would be inevitable and with Adam Cottrell going on loan to Cambridge United that is another youngster gone.

Gavin Grant has been arrested for conspiracy to murder and although that was three and a half years ago, watch the anti-Millwall media start to pursue this one.

* * *

26 August 2006, Cheltenham Town 3 – 2 Millwall

I did not think it would last. Losing 3-2 at Cheltenham means we still have not taken an away point. The referee was up to his old tricks again though. A dodgy penalty and Pidgeley getting sent off for deliberate handball did not help. It is good to see Williams scoring again and McInnes has got off the mark so I suppose it is not all doom and gloom but we're still at the bottom of the table.

Good to hear that the club are going to appeal against Pidgeley's red card but knowing our luck they'll turn it down. Come on it won't happen twice.

We have also taken Danny Senda, a defender, on trial with a view to signing him. He turned down a new contract at Wycombe Wanderers and we need a few good defenders at the moment so I hope he's one.

* * *

Here we are at transfer deadline day and nobody went. We signed Danny Senda on a short-term contract until January and also took a young midfield player, Liam Trotter, on a four-month loan from Ipswich. Nacho Novo went to Coventry and we tried to get Neil Harris but could not agree terms. What a shame. We could do with somebody like him back here and I was right about the appeal against Pidgeley's red card.

SEPTEMBER

2 September 2006, Millwall 0 – 0 Blackpool

A 0-0 home draw with Blackpool was not the best of starts for Senda and Trotter who both made their debuts. Senda looks pretty good but Trotter was not on the pitch long enough to make much of a judgement. It was a poor game though and Blackpool were not up to much. We must start getting things right and soon.

Brighton sacked Mark McGhee today and as we are playing them tomorrow I suppose that can only mean one thing. Still we have signed a new striker, Chris Zebroski, who is supposed to be pretty quick and he is six feet two inches tall, and only nineteen years old. Seems he got the push from Plymouth so I hope he can do the business like Hayles is doing for them.

* * *

9 September 2006, Millwall 0 – 1 Brighton and Hove Albion

Told you we would lose to Brighton. Okay, it was an own goal in the last couple of minutes by Elliott and we should have had at least one penalty from the three that were turned down but Brighton had ten men for most of the match. Yes, the refereeing was poor but we should have won this one. Good to see Byfield back as a substitute after his injury.

Strange thing happened after the game as everyone in the East Stand was not allowed out through the doors but had to leave by crossing the pitch to the West Stand. Wonder what that was all about.

* * *

Well we have found out why leaving on Saturday was strange. Somebody turned up with his head bleeding and the police thought the back of the East Stand was a crime scene. Turned out he had recently had brain surgery and his stitches had burst and his friends brought him to the ground because they could not get an ambulance. They knew there would be medical staff here and it seems that they managed to save his life. Bet we won't hear much about that in the media.

* * *

12 September 2006, Gillingham 2 – 1 Millwall

We lost again, this time 2-1 away at Gillingham and another late goal from Hubertz, when he was brought on as a substitute. Spackman made another load of changes with Paul Robinson taking over as captain and Fusini and Zebroski made their debuts, but if we keep making changes this side will never gel. Is this the beginning of the end for Spackman?

* * *

16 September 2006, Crewe Alexandra 1 – 0 Millwall

More changes and another defeat, this time 1-0 at Crewe. At least we were making most of the running, should have had a penalty for handball and their goalkeeper made some great saves but we need points now because we saw this happen last season and it is not good. At least Hubertz has started a game at last.

Stewart Till has gone on record as saying that Spackman has the backing of the board and the fans. I don't know what games you have been watching Stewart but the fans are very quickly losing faith in the manager and are making that known and by the way, is not the board backing the manager usually his kiss of death?

* * *

19 September 2006, English League Cup, Millwall 0 – 4 Southampton

Well we played well for the first twenty minutes and then again late in the game. Losing 0-4 at home to Southampton in the Carling Cup was a bit distorted when you look at the score line but again we gave away some easy goals. Gavin Grant would have liked a better game to make his debut in but he did play well when he came on.

The booing at the end of the game is getting louder and the 'Spackman Out' chants are too. I really can't see him staying much longer if things carry on this way. I give him to the Brentford game next Tuesday.

* * *

23 September 2006, Millwall 0 – 1 Northampton Town

The booing is getting louder and the calls for Spackman to go have now become a demonstration after losing at home again. Another silly defensive mistake gave Northampton their only chance and they took it. Yes, we hit the woodwork twice, had shots kicked off the line and their goalkeeper made some good saves but in the end it is only goals that get the points and we really do need them now.

* * *

26 September 2006, Millwall 1 – 1 Brentford

Well he did not make it to the Brentford game. Spackman was sacked last night and Donachie has taken over as caretaker for tomorrow's game against The Bees. Wonder what the result will be. More importantly who will we get as manager now as we are quickly becoming a laughing stock with all the management changes we have had in the last few seasons.

Willie Donachie.
(*Brian Tonks*)

Plenty of rumours already about who will take over the hot seat but Joe Royal is the name that keeps coming up the most. Mind you Donachie did not waste much time as caretaker manager by bringing in Danny Haynes on loan from Ipswich. It might only be for a month but the young striker looked a bit lively to me when making his debut in a side full of changes that drew 1-1 at home against Brentford, and he helped to set up Alan Dunne's equaliser.

Donachie has said he would like to take the job on permanently but he will have to do a lot more than just get a draw against Brentford to convince me, so I think the board must feel the same. Let's see how it goes in the game at Rotherham tomorrow. We must take at least a point there.

* * *

30 September 2006, Rotherham United 2 – 3 Millwall

Well how about that, not one point but three. Two goals from Haynes and another from Dunne and to think we were two goals behind as well. It has moved us up a place in the table, not a lot I know as we are still in the bottom four, but it must give the players some confidence. Keep it up Willie.

OCTOBER

The start of a new month and more paper talk about a new manager and this time Lenny Lawrence and Peter Jackson are in the frame. Whoever it is we can't afford to make another mistake.

Ray Wilkins has gone. He says it is because the contract he had was over but I'm not so sure. If he wanted the manager's job surely he would have stayed, so maybe he knows he won't be wanted by whoever takes over. Glad to see him go really because that way he can't have any influence over the way we play.

* * *

Well there is a surprise. The first team mentioned in the FA bung enquiry regarding corruption is Millwall. Good job they issued a statement to say we did nothing wrong but that is another black mark that will be put against us and never forgotten by the media.

* * *

7 October 2010, Carlisle United 1 – 2 Millwall

Wake me up because I must be dreaming. Another away win, this time 1-2 at Carlisle and Dunne just can't seem to stop scoring and nice to see Hubertz back on the score sheet. Marvin Elliott took over as captain from the injured Robinson and he certainly deserves it.

Looks like our luck might be changing too as Carlisle missed a penalty and should have had another one when Craig handled but do I care. Not on your life.

More names in the management frame, this time Andy Hessenthaler and Dave Penney. Neither of them has set the world alight before and I think we need somebody who wants to prove himself as a manager. Maybe that could be Donachie.

Stewart Till says the rumours about Peter Jackson are not true but maybe he is saying that because Huddersfield want money for him.

* * *

14 October 2006, Millwall 1 – 0 Bournemouth

Another win, so it was only 1-0 and Bournemouth hit the post before we scored but Hackett took the goal well. This is the first time that we have had the same starting eleven and the same substitutions in consecutive matches so that must say something.

We have drawn Bournemouth at home in the Johnstone's Paint Trophy in a couple of weeks time. That should be good pointer to whether we've progressed or not.

Stewart Till is now saying that he has not spoken to anyone about the manager vacancy. Why not? And Shefki Kuqi's brother, Njazi, is training with us. If he scores goals like his brother he might be worth taking on.

* * *

22 October 2006, Swansea City 2 – 0 Millwall

Oh no, we must have been doing something right because we were given a really poor referee to stop us from moving out of the bottom four. I suppose we did not really play that well and losing 2-0 at Swansea is not all that bad but the first goal should never have stood and some of the decisions the referee made bordered on the ludicrous. Just when I thought things were going our way.

There is also a rumour that we might take Leon Knight on loan. I hope not because I don't think he is that good a striker and he could be trouble. Still, I suppose we need somebody as Danny Haynes goes back to Ipswich now.

What a surprise, Dennis Wise taking over at Leeds. Okay, maybe that's a bit cynical but that must have been the worse kept secret since Bates went there and Wise was always going to end up as their manager. Good luck to them but I hope they realise that they will be digging themselves an even bigger debt hole than they are already in.

* * *

It has been a quiet week but it seems like Darren Byfield might play some part in tomorrow's game and with May and Brighton a couple of weeks away at least things might start looking up on the player front.

We will see what happens tomorrow, which is also the day for the FA Cup draw. I wonder who we'll get.

* * *

28 October 2006, Millwall 1 – 1 Port Vale

What a start to the day with the news that De Savary has resigned and Rabbatts has taken over as Chair of Millwall PLC. Maybe he heard that the planning permission for the regeneration plans he had would not be granted but I suppose he'll have his own story.

We should have beaten Port Vale quite easily and they really got away with a 1-1 draw. Zebroski took his goal well and their goal looked offside although Shaw must start to think about hoofing the ball away in those positions rather than giving it away to the opposition by trying to play the ball out of defence. Mind you we had enough chances. Their goal lived a charmed life and we could easily have scored four or five.

We drew Havant and Waterlooville away in the FA Cup so that should be interesting. We often have trouble against non-league opposition so let's hope this won't be another banana skin.

* * *

31 October 2006, Johnstone's Paint Trophy, Millwall 2 – 0 Bournemouth

Well that was a surprise, hearing that Ben May was on the bench before the start of the game against Bournemouth tonight. A good 2-0 win as well and Williams and May as scorers has a familiar ring about it. Ben scored with his first touch and showed what we have been missing. Yes it might have been the Johnstone's Paint Trophy but a win is a win and let's hope they carry that over to the game at Tranmere on Friday.

The only discouraging thing was picking up another two injuries. Craig has a dislocated shoulder and Mawene an injured knee. We certainly get those injury problems here, one back, two out.

NOVEMBER

3 November 2006, Tranmere Rovers 3 – 1 Millwall

Not the way things had been planned losing 3-1. Hackett scored a great goal and we had one in the first five minutes not given as well that definitely crossed the line. We really should have scored more than once as we had so many chances but those old defensive problems keep occurring. I'm really not sure about Shaw. Still at least Donachie showed he has the courage to change things when he made two substitutions on the half hour mark and then another just after the start of the second half. Come on the board, give him the job permanently.

We have drawn Brighton at home in the next round of the Johnstone's Paint Trophy so let's see how much we've progressed since we played them last.

It seems like the police are causing problems with our FA Cup game against Havant, nothing new there then. They have already moved it to Monday night and then to Fratton Park so who knows what will happen next.

Donachie says he is looking for loan players to help out while we have so many injured players in the squad; there are twelve out at the moment. I can't wait for some of them to get back but I wonder who he will get, if anyone, to help in the meantime.

* * *

Just heard that the club lost £4 million last season but that is £1 million better than the season before. Well with everything that has gone on over the last two seasons I suppose that is not too bad. Now all we need is the side to start winning and moving up the table and maybe we can start to bring more fans in and increase the gate receipts. We certainly need it.

* * *

Jody Morris is such a fool, fancy driving the wrong way down a street in south London and being drunk at the same time. I know the club say they will stand by him and help him but in truth they could not say much else. I wonder if his contract will be renewed when it runs out at the end of the season. Wouldn't it be funny if Dennis Wise took him back to Leeds? Nah! That will never happen.

I like the idea of special gates at the stadium entrance. Hopefully it will match the montage on the two stands. Add that to the pictures and walls being painted inside the stands and things are looking up. Wish we could start getting the team to go the same way.

Well if we win tomorrow's game against Havant we play Bradford away in the next round. Let's wait to see what happens tomorrow as we must not get carried away.

* * *

13 November 2006, English FA Cup, Millwall 2 – 1 Havant and Waterlooville
Well we won 2-1 but we made hard work of it, which I suppose was always likely to be the case as they really did have nothing to lose, well except a lot of money. There were more police there than there were Millwall fans and that is not the way for things to go. Another goal from May and a cracker from Dunne that helped stop us slipping on a banana skin of a game. I hope that does not start going to Dunne's head like it did last season though.

I can't believe Zebroski has got five yellow cards already. That puts him out of the Forest game so we really do need to get Byfield and May back to full fitness quickly.

* * *

Well I suppose we have been having a problem or two with the defence so getting a defender in on loan is not a bad move, but I thought we would get an experienced bruiser in, not a young one. Welcome Charlie Lee. Hope you are as good as Spurs and we think you are.

* * *

18 November 2006, Millwall 2 – 2 Doncaster Rovers
Well Charlie, you look good to me. Shame that there are still problems with the defence but maybe you can help to sort it out. Mind you the problem

seems more to do with other players defending than the defensive players themselves. Still the 2-2 draw with Doncaster has moved us out of the bottom four, yippee, and Mark McCammon did not score.

Byfield's goal was fairly simple although he should have had a second before they took the lead again. Hackett's was a cracker. He does not score simple goals does he? Hope he stays fit for the rest of the season now.

However, I am not sure that the 4-3-3 system that was used in this game works well. There were lots of problems in midfield and that helped with them scoring both their goals.

Well the board have decided to give Donachie the manager's job on a permanent basis and about time too, having said that, he'll probably start losing now. That is sod's law I suppose. I still think we can get out of trouble but I'm only expecting a mid-table finish.

Two days in charge and Donachie is saying that up to ten players will go, because they are not up to the job. He also says he'll bring in some new ones but who will come with us struggling again?

Stewart Till is saying that there is no need to sell anybody but if the right offer came in then who knows. I suppose that means saying goodbye to Marvin Elliott and Alan Dunne as both their contracts are up at the end of this season and probably Ben May, Lenny Pidgeley and Chris Hackett, as they are the ones who will bring in the money.

* * *

25 November 2006, Nottingham Forest 3 – 1 Millwall
Told you, Donachie's first game in charge and we lose at Nottingham Forest. Maybe the 3-1 score line flattered them but we could not capitalise on May's early goal and as usual our defending helped them score in the second half. Here we go, back into the bottom four.

* * *

28 November 2006, Johnstone's Paint Trophy, Millwall 1 – 1 Brighton and Hove Albion (Brighton won on penalties)
Well we should be in the next round of the Johnstone's Paint Trophy. We were winning easily after Robinson put us in front and Brighton only had ten men – again. Once again we defended badly and gave a goal away right at the end and then we could not score from the spot in the penalty shoot-out. Byfield's was awful, Lee's was well saved and there was a lot of pressure on Whitbread but at least he had the guts to take one.

Well taken penalties by Senda and Zebroski and two good saves from Day but why did not May and Hackett take one?

DECEMBER

1 December 2006, English FA Cup, Bradford City 0 – 0 Millwall

I suppose a 0-0 draw at Bradford City was not a bad result in the end, especially as they hit the woodwork three times, but then again we should have scored a few ourselves. Are we going backwards again? Still, at least we are in the draw for the next round of the cup on Sunday and although we could do without the extra game, who knows. If we draw a big side the extra money will come in handy.

* * *

Stoke, we drew Stoke. Oh well two wins needed before we get a big side. Still we have to win the game against Huddersfield on Tuesday to get our confidence on the rise again and then two games against Bradford. That will be interesting.

* * *

5 December 2006, Millwall 0 – 0 Huddersfield Town

0-0 against Huddersfield was not the most inspiring of games. A very drab first half and we were playing 4-3-3 but when we changed to 4-4-2 at the start of the second half it was much better. Morais certainly livened things up, replacing Zebroski at half time. We should have scored a few but Huddersfield's delaying tactics didn't help either.

Shame to see Braniff go but things never did work out for him. Having his contract cancelled at least will help him. He is going back to Ireland first before he looks for a club. Hope he finds himself one soon.

* * *

9 December 2006, Millwall 2 – 0 Bradford City

Wow. What a great performance against Bradford. If we play them like this in the cup on Tuesday they have no chance. We should have had a lot more goals than Morais' early opener and Byfield's penalty. Playing 4-4-2 is certainly best for us. We will miss Hackett on Tuesday night but at least we're out of the bottom four.

* * *

12 December 2006, English FA Cup, Millwall 1 – 0 Bradford City (aet)

What a difference a few days make. We were unrecognisable to the side that beat Bradford on Saturday; mind you their defenders certainly want to score for us. They tried it on Saturday and had a few goes today before they managed to put the ball in the net for our extra time winner tonight. I am not complaining but again we were poor until extra time. Must be more consistent is all I will say.

* * *

What is going on? As soon as we reach the third round, Stoke and their local plod decide to change our game to Friday night. Once again we are not consulted and our support suffers. Somebody needs to look at this and they would if we were Manchester United or Chelsea or a club like that but we are Millwall so who cares?

At least we have extended Charlie Lee's loan until the end of January and that is good. Maybe we can try to keep him until the end of the season after that.

Goodbye number two, Derek McInnes, another cancelled contract and he is going back to Scotland. I wonder who the other eight will be.

* * *

16 December 2006, Bristol City 1 – 0 Millwall

Fifteen seconds, that is all it took to lose the game at Bristol City. Still at least we had a go changing from 4-4-2 to 4-3-3 and 4-2-4. We just can't score at the moment and that is not good. What is good was the fact that not a single Millwall player got booked. The referee must have forgotten we were one of the sides on the pitch. The bad news is that we are second from bottom again.

Dean Pooley was the third to go and another contract cancelled. I know he only played the once but he looked all right to me, but what do I know. Obviously Donachie didn't fancy him. Well three down, seven to go.

* * *

22 December 2006, Millwall 0 – 1 Scunthorpe United

Scunthorpe are top of the table but they didn't look much to me. Okay, we lost 1-0 and it is typical that Steve Torpey had to score the goal. Why is it that ex-players score so often against their old clubs? Still, it was naive play that gave the ball away for them to score, but we should have won by a cricket score. Byfield alone missed enough to have won three games.

Good to see Neil Ardley back in the side. He made a lot of difference and with Dunne signing a three-year contract before the game I suppose the omens are good. Wonder why Elliott is not getting chased for a signature on a new contract like Dunne was. I suppose it is a sign that he must be going.

* * *

26 December 2006, Brentford 1 – 4 Millwall

Jingle bells, jingle bells, jingle all the way, oh what fun it is to see Millwall win 4-1 away. I still can't believe it. Two from Hubertz, one from Robinson and a Byfield penalty – don't like that silly run-up of his – and we are out of the bottom four and with a point gap. Keep this up, beat Northampton and we are away.

I wonder who the tough tackling midfield player is that Donachie says he wants to buy. He also says that he has had bids for Robinson, Whitbread, Phillips and Zebroski but turned them all down so they are not in the ten. It is interesting that there was no mention of bids for Elliott or Williams.

* * *

What nonsense to abandon the Northampton game with twenty minutes left, and we were winning 0-1 at the time. Why is it that Hubertz's 'goal' won't count but the two bookings we got do? Now we are back in the bottom four again and have a defensive problem with Senda injured. We must beat Gillingham on Monday.

JANUARY

1 January 2007, Millwall 4 – 1 Gillingham
Two 4-1 wins in a row, I must be dreaming, and to think that Gillingham went in front as well. I take it all back about Byfield, well for now anyway, it was a great hat-trick and Zebroski took his goal well. Could have been five when May hit the bar. Now we are back up to nineteenth in the table, and we need to keep going that way.

Derek McInnes has joined St Johnstone; Trotter has gone back to Ipswich (don't know why we bothered); Alan Brookes and Adam Cotterell have gone as well, although both did not play a first team game; and Lee goes back to Spurs at the end of next week, although he wasn't in the original ten. Well that just leaves four to go and I wonder who they will be.

* * *

5 January 2007, English FA Cup, Stoke City 2 – 0 Millwall
Friday night and it must be an away FA Cup game. Stoke were lucky to come away with a 2-0 win as I thought it was going to end 0-0 until the ball flew in off of Elliott and we were chasing the equaliser when they scored their second. We did not play well though so let's get back to the league and away from the wrong end of it.

I wonder what truth there is in the rumours that Neil Harris and Robbie Ryan might re-join the club. We will just have to wait and see.

* * *

13 January 2007, Brighton and Hove Albion 0 – 1 Millwall
Super Neil Harris signed today on an eighteen-month contract and we got him for free. Hope everything works out for him and we don't see the demise of a hero. Danny Senda also signed a new contract for the same length of time.

Neil Harris returns to The Den. (*Brian Tonks*)

Well Harris played the whole game in the 0-1 win at Brighton and although it was Byfield who scored, he made a telling contribution. We have got to keep this up now and not lose sight of getting well away from the bottom, then who knows.

Nothing much going on in the transfer window but Donachie says there will be a lot of movement in the next two weeks. I bet that will be out and not in but I suppose we will have to wait and see.

* * *

20 January 2007, Millwall 4 – 0 Rotherham United

Told you it would be out. Filipe Morais has gone on loan for the rest of the season to St Johnstone, joining Derek McInnes there. I wonder if we will see him next season. Doubt it.

Well you could not have written that script and if you did then nobody would believe it possible. Harris opens the scoring in his first match back at The Den to break Sheringham's league scoring record, so now he is on ninety-four and needs just thirteen more to become the highest goal scorer ever at the club. It could not happen to a nicer bloke.

His goal was the first of a stunning 4-0 win over Rotherham. Zebroski took his goal well and the second of Byfield's two was amazing. It must have been from all of forty yards. Can we have him booked every week if it means he is going to score goals like that just afterwards?

It was good to see Morris and Brighton back as subs. I can't wait for Brighton to get match fit but I am not sure about Morris as we have plenty of midfield players now.

* * *

23 January 2007, Northampton Town 3 – 0 Millwall

It is not fair. Winning 1-0 when the first game at Northampton was abandoned, we end up losing the replayed match 3-0 and get Dunne sent off in the process. Mind you having him suspended for three games will help us I think because he either plays for Millwall or plays for himself and when he is in 'Dunne

Neil Harris scores in his first game back. (*Brian Tonks*)

mode' he is awful and the trouble is he can switch at any time in a game, which I think makes him unreliable.

Lots of rumours that we are about to bring in Darren Currie from Ipswich. Now I think he is a good player but don't we have enough wingers. Still I suppose it is that Donachie-Ipswich connection working again.

Zoom's gone to Brighton on loan for the rest of the season. Shame because I liked him. Well in theory there is only one more of Donachie's ten to go so who will it be I wonder, would not mind it being Morris now he is fit.

* * *

27 January 2007, Scunthorpe 3 – 0 Millwall

Well he started with Morris and Brighton in the game at Scunthorpe so that is my wish out of the window. Mind you they were both well short of match fitness, which is only to be expected I suppose.

I thought we were having a good game but fell apart again and losing 3-0 did not really paint a true picture of the match. Yeovil next and I don't expect anything from that game either.

Well Michael Bostwick has gone to Rushden and Diamonds so that is the ten. I know he never featured in the first team so maybe that is why, still nobody coming in and only two days of the transfer window left.

* * *

One day to go and we have signed Dave Brammer on a free from Stoke on a two-and-a-half-year contract. Donachie says this is the midfield player he wanted and we needed so we'll find out at the end of the week whether he is right or not.

* * *

Last day of the transfer window and nobody else joined the club but Gavin Grant has gone on loan to Grays. I suppose that's the end of the Darren Currie move to us then.

FEBRUARY

3 February 2007, Yeovil Town 0 – 1 Millwall

I was right about Morris then. Donachie has told him he can go out on loan for the rest of the season if he can find a club to take him. Now that will be interesting.

Dave Brammer made his debut at Yeovil and we win 0-1 thanks to a goal from Ben May. We had to do a lot of defending though and I thought that Phillips, in for the suspended Shaw, had a great game in the middle of the defence with Robinson, and Brammer certainly played his part. Up to seventeenth in the table now so let's hope we can keep it up.

Oh no! Donachie has been nominated as the manager of the month and Byfield as player of the month for the division. Let's hope they both fail to win it as we don't want to be brought down by 'The Curse'.

* * *

10 February 2007, Millwall 2 – 1 Chesterfield

Well we made hard work of the 2-1 win over Chesterfield but it is another three points and we're up to fourteenth. Byfield took his goal well and Hubertz scored a great one, especially as it was the winner. However, we must stop slackening off during games and giving the opposition something to go for.

Not sure about the Byfield penalty that was turned down. Maybe he should just get on with the game and stop playing 'Fancy Dan' stuff because he goes over much too easily.

It was nice to see the old players back for Dockers Day and some of the old Dockers that were supporters and what a good idea of Peter Garston to do it. That is one reason for having a fan on the board. Well done.

The rumour about Darren Currie is back, this time to take him on loan for the rest of the season. We'll have to wait and see but I don't think it will happen. It is shame about Ben May. Just when he was starting to get back into some sort of form then injury puts him out for another 4-6 weeks.

We're still looking at players to take on. As well as Damien Scannell at Fisher we're looking at Claude Scanla who was at Watford and James Frayne, once of Liverpool. I'm not sure if we really want to take on players at the moment that might not be up to it. We seem to have enough of those already.

* * *

17 February 2007, Oldham Athletic 1 – 2 Millwall

I didn't think we would take a point at Oldham, especially as they are (or should that be were?) the league leaders but what do I know. 1-0 down and on comes Williams who scores with his first touch and Hubertz, who has a shot handled and gets a penalty, which Byfield puts away.

Donachie certainly knows how to make changes at the right time and we're up to twelfth in the table. Bring on the Orient.

* * *

20 February 2007, Millwall 2 – 5 Leyton Orient

What a shambles. Three down in twelve minutes, finally losing 2-5 and one of those two was an own goal. Mind you Hubertz scored a good one when he came on.

Yes Harris, Senda and Phillips all hit the bar but our defending was abysmal and that is probably the last time Phillips will play in the first team, and although he wasn't entirely to blame he takes most of it.

Mind you the refereeing was atrocious. Call him a Premiership referee. I've seen better on a Sunday morning. Having said that I wish Byfield would cut out the diving and stop the posing. He would be a much better player if he did. Well let's call it a bad day at the office and put in a better display at Blackpool.

* * *

24 February 2007, Blackpool 0 – 1 Millwall
Told you Phillips would not play again as he was the only change from Tuesday night with Robinson coming back and what happens – we win. A 0-1 win does it for me and Brammer's first for the club was brilliant. Like to see him get more of those, he really does look a good buy.

MARCH

Oh no! Donachie is up for manager of the month again. Mind you he didn't get it the last time and we lost 2-5 so maybe if he wins it we'll go on and get promotion (only joking, please don't let him win it).

* * *

3 March 2007, Millwall 2 – 0 Cheltenham Town
Well he didn't and we beat Cheltenham 2-0. Byfield scores again and Tom Brighton gets his first for the club. Shame we haven't seen much of him this season so let's hope he stays injury free for the rest of it.

Goodbye Maurice Ross, off for a trial in Norway with Viking FC. He was never going to get back into the side here so let's hope it does well there.

Wow! Money coming into the club, £5 million to be exact, so that should help with our £3 million losses. So we now have American owners in Chestnut Hill Ventures and an American chairman in John Berylson but who cares if it makes the club more secure. De Savary put in some more as well and so have others.

However, I hope it's not just to take it out again when the regeneration thing happens, which I'm sure it will eventually.

Good move by Willie to bring in Colin West to coach the strikers. Maybe we'll see Byfield stay on his feet a bit more.

Well the shipping out of players has started with Gavin Grant having his loan extended to the end of the season, Maurice Ross passing his trial and being given a free, and Marvin Williams going on loan to Torquay.

With 'Sport City' having been given the go-ahead we'll just have to wait and see what happens. Ever the optimist I hope it doesn't have any effect on the football club, except for the money that it will bring in.

You can tell it is getting near to season ticket purchase time with rumours about a Premiership striker or two. As usual I expect it will be either a dead beat nobody or nobody at all. I certainly won't hold my breath waiting for him to turn up.

* * *

10 March 2007, Millwall 2 – 0 Carlisle United
Two goals for Neil Harris to beat Carlisle and his wife gave birth to a daughter on Monday. What a way to celebrate. That takes him over the 100 mark and next season he is bound to take the all goals record from Sheringham. I'm glad he scored because I had a funny feeling he would never score again.

* * *

13 March 2007, Millwall 2 – 2 Crewe Alexandra
Hubertz to the rescue again with another late goal and another one from Byfield gave us a 2-2 draw with Crewe. We must stop giving goals away but the fact that we're just four points away from a play-off place means I should not grumble. I still don't think we'll get one though but we can still dream.

Three out, one in, Nathan Ashton has arrived on loan from Charlton. I suppose we need some cover at left back but will he be another Trotter or a Haynes?

* * *

17 March 2007, Bournemouth 1 – 0 Millwall
What a poor game we had at Bournemouth. Losing 1-0 wasn't the point; we did not even have a shot on target. If we want that play-off spot we will need to do better than that.

Glad Donachie has been given a new two-year contract. He deserves it and come to that so do the other members of the backroom staff. Come on board put your money where your mouth is.

I hope going on loan to Oxford will help Zebroski. He is a willing horse but still has a lot to learn. However, let's hope that Ryan Smith does not need to learn much. We will see if he gets a game during his month's loan with us.

Goodbye Mark Phillips. Your loan to Darlington will be the start of the long goodbye, especially as we have brought in Chris Casement from Ipswich to take your place. I can't understand it but again I suppose we need the cover at this stage of the season and it gives Willie a chance to have a look at some young players for next season as well.

* * *

24 March 2007, Port Vale 2 – 0 Millwall

We are ten points behind the play-off positions now we have lost 2-0 to Port Vale and that is just about where I thought we would end up. I know we hit the woodwork a couple of times but when we dominate games like that we really should make the most of it. It is goals that win matches not domination.

At least we got a look at Ryan Smith when Brighton got injured (again) and he looks the business. I hope he continues like that for the rest of his loan period.

The E.G.M. with the board sounded like it could bring trouble to the club but it seems like things have been sorted out, for now anyway, so let's get on with the job in hand and see how things develop.

* * *

31 March 2007, Millwall 2 – 0 Swansea City

Playing Swansea was like playing a training match, it was that easy and we should have had a lot more than the two goals Robinson and Harris scored. Ryan Smith looks like he could be something special. Can we keep him please?

With a big game coming up against Forest next week, making sure we did not pick up any silly injuries makes sense. Except we did with Byfield getting injured in the first minute and with May and Brighton out for the rest of the season we are looking at a striker shortage. Maybe we should recall Williams from Torquay.

APRIL

Things have got worse as it seems that Byfield will be out for the rest of the season as well now, so that just leaves Harris and Hubertz. Get on the phone Willie and do it right now.

I must have the gift of telepathy as Williams is back. Thank goodness for that as having only inexperienced cover now would blow our slim promotion hope right out of the water.

That also goes for the backroom staff, Pat Holland and Kevin Dearden have all been offered new contracts and Holland is now officially the assistant manager. I wonder if I can telepathically send messages to the team and also the opposition.

* * *

7 April 2007, Millwall 1 – 0 Nottingham Forest

Neil Harris scores the only goal of the game, who else would it be? We also hit the bar and the post and although they hit a post as well, Forest were well and truly beaten.

What a great game it was, especially for Harris after all the taunting he got from the Forest fans. Just think he has scored more for us since he came back than in the two years he was with them. There must be something in that.

* * *

9 April 2007, Doncaster Rovers 1 – 2 Millwall

Behind at Doncaster and it is Williams and Hubertz to the rescue again. Up another place and just nine points away from the playoff places but I think it will all be too much with just four games left. Still who knows? Let's see what happens against Tranmere on Saturday.

Goodbye Ken Brown and hello Andy Ambler. Brown going won't be a bad move, especially where the fans are concerned and if Ambler makes us as profitable as he did Fulham it will be a smart move. However, I'm still a bit concerned that all this has a lot to do with the regeneration. Am I getting a bit nervous? You bet your life I am, but the season tickets for next season are bought so let's kick on from here.

* * *

14 April 2007, Millwall 2 – 2 Tranmere Rovers

We do like shooting ourselves in the foot don't we? A 2-2 draw with Tranmere did neither side any favours and I must say Alan Dunne took both of his goals well. Yet once again poor refereeing let us down as a third goal from Byfield (glad his injury wasn't as bad as first thought) should have stood. Referees should wait just a bit and see what develops before giving free kicks and the decision then, plus two similar ones in the first half, cost us the game.

Charlton have recalled Ashton and as he never got passed the subs bench I can understand why. However, Smith has had his loan increased until the end of the season and I hope that does not mean that some other club signs him in the closed season after we show what he can do (as happened with Huckerby all those years ago). If we can't sign him permanently then try for a season loan. He must not slip through our net.

* * *

21 April 2007, Huddersfield Town 4 – 2 Millwall

Here we go again, back to joke defending. Losing 4-2 at Huddersfield is not the point, we need to stop making poor defensive errors or we'll be in this division for longer than we want to be. Good goals from Byfield and Dunne though, and are we seeing the start of some sort or partnership between Smith and Dunne? That is three goals Dunne has scored in two weeks and all from passes from Smith after one of his mazy runs.

Chris Casement has gone back to Ipswich without getting further than the bench. I really don't understand the point of taking a player on loan and then not using him. Yes, it adds a bit of pressure to somebody else but if that is the only reason to bring somebody in then maybe the point is lost on me.

Congratulations to Richard Shaw on winning the player of the year award and by a large percentage. However, I get really disappointed with the number of actual votes cast. Are our fans really that apathetic or is it that the voting slips don't get handed in by the stewards?

* * *

28 April 2007, Millwall 1 – 0 Bristol City

Well we stopped Bristol City's promotion party and it was a fairly easy 1-0 win. Robinson took his goal like a twenty-goal-a-season striker and the game had a great atmosphere, it was a great game and a great win. Wish we could get something like that for most of the season. Not sure about the new kit though.

MAY

5 May 2007, Bradford City 2 – 2 Millwall

The authorities can't let a season go by without punishing us for something can they? We are already going to get a big fine for the number of bookings we have had this season and now we're charged over the incident at the end of the game with Huddersfield. It'll be interesting to see what happens with this one.

Last game of the season and it showed. We didn't want to know really and I suppose a 2-2 draw would have been fine at any other time of the season but we should have won this one.

Byfield and Craig took their goals well I suppose and it was good to see May back. In fact, if we can keep this squad together and a few good additions made, we could be knocking on the promotion door next season. I just wish the first half of this season had been like the second one. Still I guess that everyone associated with the club feels the same.

Well now it is time to look out for who comes in and maybe more importantly, who goes. It should be an interesting closed season.

CHAPTER THREE

THE GREAT ESCAPE
SEASON 2007/2008

CLOSED SEASON

Well it is nice to see some commitment to the club. First of all Willie Donachie moves from Ipswich to live here in London, at least he can show the players his commitment. That must be good for their moral and hopefully help them become more committed to the club if they fall short on that somewhere.

Then we get John Berylson upsetting the Football League about the way Leeds went into administration and losing the ten points they were deducted from last season and not this one. At least that loophole has been closed now but Leeds should have started this season ten points short. I hope they get what is coming to them anyway. As they say, what goes around comes around.

Richard Shaw has shown his commitment by signing a new one-year contract so now let's see whom else stays and more importantly who goes.

Just seen Charlie Lee has gone to Peterborough. I thought he was a pretty good player while he was here on loan and could have done a job for us. I still don't understand why players that come here on loan are rarely signed by us and go somewhere else.

* * *

Well the rumour factory has started and we're supposed to be bringing in Danny Spiller and Michael Flynn from Gillingham. I can't say I remember much about either of them so that might say something. Nothing concrete about either of them so we'll just have to wait and see.

Another striker and midfield player rumoured to be joining the club as well and this time they're both from Spurs, Lee Barnard and Jamie O'Hara. These two are supposed to be coming on loans unlike the two from Gillingham who are to be permanent deals, like I have said before only time will tell.

* * *

Now another striker comes into play, this time Gary Alexander from Leyton Orient and again on a permanent deal. He looked good when he played against us and scored twice so who knows? He will certainly add some competition for places up front if he came.

More good news for the club, it has been praised for efforts made in the kick out racism campaign. It is about time we got some recognition for the good things about this club and not hammered by the bad things, which I am glad to say is getting less and less.

Goodbye Adam Cottrell, we never saw you play so it is hard to say what I think about you and goodbye Jody Morris. Never saw you play much either, at least not very well most of the time, so I suppose I have to be glad you're gone. All the rest of the squad, including those sent out on loan last season have been retained so it will be interesting to see who, if anyone, goes now, especially when and if we bring new faces in.

Once again the rumour factory is talking about Darren Currie coming to the club. Well he did not seem very committed to Millwall when we tried for him last season and he went to Derby, now they don't want him he seems to have had a change of heart. That does not sound very committed to me except for commitment to himself.

* * *

Well, the first two have joined and it is Alexander and Spiller. So we have a striker and a midfield player, will anyone go? Marvin Elliott is the obvious candidate but he's been offered a new contract – does he want to stay and fight for a place or go and fight for a place? We'll find out soon I suppose.

We won a seeded place in the Carling Cup first round draw and then got Northampton away. We have also been made third favourites with the bookies for promotion after Nottingham Forest and Leeds. Hope we can live up to expectations, I think we can.

* * *

League fixtures out today and we start with a difficult trip to Doncaster, then the game at Northampton and then our first home match against Cheltenham. By then we should see what type of start to the season we are going to have. I can't wait.

Well done Teddy Sheringham for getting an MBE but fancy endangering that by being arrested for giving false information to the police about driving. See that is what happens when you get involved with West Ham.

I have just seen that Barry Cogan has gone to Gillingham so you know what that means. Yes, I know he looked a bit lightweight when he was with us but it still plays on your mind.

Another player joins the club. Scott Barron comes from Ipswich and is another left sided midfield player, so I suppose that means we have given up on Ryan Smith.

Well maybe I'm wrong about Smith as there is still a lot of talk about him coming here but I'll just wait and see. There is also talk of Mark Phillips going to either Darlington or Leyton Orient and worse than that Tony Craig to Crystal Palace, not another one.

* * *

Well Craig's gone to Palace and although there was no mention of how much we got for him, some of it, at least, went to bring in Andy Frampton from Brentford. Another left footer and a full back at that, so we have covered the vacancy left by Craig. According to Steven Till there are possibly two more players to come and then Donachie is happy with the squad but I think there will still be a few more players leaving.

* * *

Well that is Darren Currie out of the picture as he has joined Luton. I never thought that he wanted to join us in the first place unless we were the only club he could get. He was never going to be committed like Donachie wanted so I'm not bothered about not getting him.

We got Ryan Smith so that is good news; although I think it is a shame that we will lose Poul Hubertz as he gave his all for the club. He might not have been the best in the world but he tried and he was our second top scorer for last season. Still, I was finding it difficult to see where he was going to fit in.

Sending Marvin Williams out on loan next season might help bring him along, although it could well be the last we see of him as well. I'm not surprised to see Philips, Morais and Grant not given squad numbers for next season and although Zebroski might be worth hanging onto for another year, together with Mawene and Bakayogo, it is goodbye to them as well.

What a shame about David Amoo going to Liverpool. If he had stayed with us he would have got a chance to play first team football and as I always say, 'If you're good enough you'll get to the top clubs.' You would think he would have learnt from Cherno Samba doing the same thing. Still I wish him well.

I have just seen that Marc Bircham has gone to Yeovil. I wonder if he'll paint his face green and white and say he was always a fan. He's still got a lion on his arm though. Marvin Elliott hasn't been given a squad number so I suppose he will definitely be going. He's another one who has started to believe his own hype, like others, who shall remain nameless, before him. Oh well, he could have developed here but again I wish him well wherever he ends up.

* * *

Started the pre-season games and lost 2-1 at Dundee. Glad to see Ben May scoring goals again. It should be interesting to see who gets the starting positions up front this season.

We also played a player on trial, Toumani Diagouraga, who we're looking to take on a year's loan from Watford. The Frenchman is a midfield player and Donachie is comparing him to Elliott. Well I suppose we'll have to wait and see if we take him on.

* * *

Oh great! Lenny Pidgeley has broken his toe and will be out for six weeks, and with Preston Edwards injured as well we could start the season with just one goalkeeper. Here we go again especially as Tom Brighton still is not fully fit.

Mark Phillips is having a trial with MK Dons, Chris Zebroski is having one with Hereford and Ross Gaynor with Welling, so we could be saying goodbye to them soon. At least we've won a friendly, even if it was behind closed doors, as we beat Clyde 2-1 with goals from May and Ardley.

* * *

Now we've lost 1-0 at Falkirk. Still this was well short of what should be our first choice side and the 1-1 draw with Motherwell was more like it. Another Brammer screamer and I hope he gets a few of them this season. Now it is back south of the border and a few games here before the real thing starts.

* * *

Oh no! Marvin Williams has gone to Yeovil. So that's two goals against us when we play them if the ex-player theory comes true.

What is it about Hampshire police and us? Last season was the FA Cup match against Havant and Waterlooville that they spoilt and now it is the friendly at Aldershot. Now the game has been called off. Why do they want so many police there and charge silly prices for it. They should take a leaf out Kent police book. They are all right about the friendly at Ebbsfleet tonight.

* * *

Maybe the Kent police knew something as we lost 2-0 but there was really something wrong with the side tonight. Can't put my finger on it but if we play like that when the season starts then we'll struggle.

Another goal against us as Don Hutchinson has joined Luton. Hope that is all a lot of tosh or we're in big trouble next season.

Willie Donachie must be reading my thoughts as he's decided not to take on the Frenchman we had on trial as he's no better than what we have already. I suppose that means he'll go somewhere else and play against us and score. I must get this idea out of my system.

* * *

Played Aldershot behind closed doors at The Den, that is one in the eye for the boys in blue and the other boys in blue won 2-0 with goals from Spiller and Hackett.

There must be something in the West Country air. First Williams goes there and now Marvin Elliott has gone to Bristol City. I think he finally got too big in the head and thought he was better than he really is. Still I wish him well and maybe it will bring him on again. Filipe Morais has gone to Hibernian. Good move for him and I think he'll do well there.

* * *

Lost 1-0 to Southampton, I'll be glad when theses pre-season friendly games are over but I suppose they have to be played to build match fitness.

Lindley Catering, the new caterers, need to make things better at the kiosks around the ground with both what's on offer and what they charge for it. If they make themselves too pricey they'll soon come a cropper. They say they'll make improvements but we'll see.

Big rumours about Darren Byfield and Richard Shaw having a training ground bust up before the Ebbsfleet match so that would explain the display. Seems like Donachie has had enough of 'Baby Boy' and he could be on his way out. That would also explain why he hasn't been seen in any matches since then. Chris Zebroski has gone on loan to Torquay until the end of the year and that should help bring him on. Gavin Grant has been found not guilty in his murder trial. That will be a weight off of his mind and maybe he can settle down and start playing now.

* * *

Our first bit of silverware in a long time, with the Unity in the Community Cup. We won by beating Sierra Leone 2-1. Goals came from Harris and Alexander. Well that's the end of the friendly games, so bring on the real thing. No Byfield but Shaw played so maybe those rumours are right.

Byfield is having a meeting with Donachie and Till. I'd like to be a fly on the wall for that one. I think we've seen the last of him but you never know. If he was to go, why not keep Hubertz or bring back Danny Haynes from Ipswich?

There are two more ex-players to come up against this season with Curtis Weston and Leon Constantine both going to Leeds. Glad the League decided to make them keep their fifteen-point deduction for the way they have gone

Squad for start of season 2007/2008. *(Chris Bethell)*

about things during the closed season. That will teach them and anybody else not to bend the rules.

* * *

I'm getting ex-player syndrome now that Poul Hubertz has signed for Northampton. I really need the season to start and get my mind on something else.

At last the club have admitted there's a problem with Byfield and it's his attitude and commitment. Could have told them that myself as he really is a selfish so-and-so. I guess we'll find out what will finally happen over the next few weeks.

AUGUST

11 August 2007, Doncaster Rovers 0 – 0 Millwall

We didn't get a bye from the first round of the League Cup, and we've drawn Swansea away in the Johnstone's Paint Trophy this season. The 0-0 draw at Doncaster was a good result for the first game as they're bound to be one of the leading teams this season and we had a May goal disallowed (here we go again). No Byfield but Spiller, Frampton, Barron and Alexander all made their debuts.

Sammy Mawene has had his contract cancelled, which I think is a shame. He looked like a skilful player to me but never really got given a chance. I suppose Zoom goes next.

* * *

What a surprise. Not only is Zoom staying but he has been given a squad number and taken to Northampton for tonight's game. Isn't it funny how things change so quickly in the football world?

* * *

14 August 2007, English League Cup, Northampton Town 2 – 0 Millwall

Well that's us out of the Carling Cup losing 2-0 at Northampton. Hubertz didn't score but he made the second goal. We made loads of chances again, but just couldn't put them away. Hope we do better on Saturday.

Fined £30,000 and another fine of the same amount suspended because of our disciplinary record for last season. Our record will be looked at again in October but the way referees like to show yellow cards to Millwall players for almost anything won't help us at all.

Jemelia has split up with 'Baby Boy', so I wonder if it is because of the problems at The Den or the other way round. He's still isn't even training with the first team.

Why has Chris Hackett been offered to Darlington? Was it permanently or on loan? Why isn't he playing in the first team? Most fans want to see him there. I think he is probably the most talented player we have at the moment. I just can't understand it but I suppose you never know what goes on behind the scenes.

* * *

18 August 2007, Millwall 1 – 0 Cheltenham Town

Three points and our first goal, well done Danny Spiller, although we made hard work of beating Cheltenham and it could have been worse if they hadn't hit the post late on in the game. We keep making loads of chances but still not taking them. There's something missing up front and although that might be Byfield, I suppose we need to get him out of our minds and start thinking of other players to score.

Still we're up to sixth in the table and although I know it is early in the season I'd rather be there than at the bottom.

Just read that Spiller's goal was the club's 5,000th League goal. Doesn't sound much but I suppose when normally only one or two are scored in a game and often none, it would take a while to reach that number.

* * *

What a week this has been. First Chris Hackett says he will stay and fight for a place in the team. Good for him as he could have gone to Darlington. How is that for commitment to the team, Willie?

Then Gavin Grant goes on a season loan to Grays Athletic. That court case must have preyed on his mind. Still now he's been found not guilty he can get back to playing and this should help him.

Next two midfield players arrive; Jamie O'Hara on a one-month loan from Spurs and Peter Vincenti on a four-month contract from St Peters in Jersey. The question is will we use either of them? Still no news about Byfield but I'm sure he'll be gone by the end of the month.

* * *

25 August 2007, Southend United 1 – 0 Millwall

Well that is one of everything now having lost 1-0 to Southend. At least O'Hara played and he looked quite good. We must put away our chances though.

There have been enquiries for Byfield from Blackpool and Bristol City. From his point of view I suppose Bristol would be best but they only want to take him on loan so from the club's point of view money from Blackpool should take preference, I hope it does.

Donachie keeps talking about bringing in loan players but we really do need a settled squad and players coming in and out won't help us get that.

* * *

Byfield's gone to Bristol and at least we got money from them for him. I suppose they realised we would sell him to Blackpool or keep him otherwise. Now can we get a striker in to replace him please?

* * *

My request has been answered and we have brought in Jay Simpson from Arsenal until the end of the year. Only a kid but Danny Haynes was that last season and proved good so maybe Simpson will too.

SEPTEMBER

1 September 2007, Millwall 1 – 2 Huddersfield Town

Well Simpson made his debut against Huddersfield and looked like he might have something but we lost again, 1-2. Not a bad goal from Robinson but the defending or to be more precise goalkeeping was really poor. Shame Dunne's 'goal' was disallowed as we would never have dropped points then.

Looks like Portsmouth are after another two of our academy kids. Don't these youngsters ever learn or is it their parents seeing pound signs in their eyes. I bet they go if the money to us is right but we must try and stop this somehow although we can't sign them until they're sixteen so it makes it difficult to stop them being poached.

* * *

Well now we know who these Premiership strikers that Donachie was talking about are, Radzinski and Dickov. We've tried to sign Dickov for years, since he was a kid at Arsenal, and he always turned us down. He'll never come here. Good try for Radzinski but would we ever have been able to afford his wages? However, we must start scoring soon and especially the strikers we have.

* * *

4 September 2007, Johnstone's Paint Trophy, Swansea 3 – 2 Millwall
Well we are out of the Johnstone's Paint Trophy having lost 3-2 at Swansea but at least we had the goals scored by strikers, so stand up May and Simpson. Lost because of a Whitbread own goal, but it gets worse.

O'Hara was sent off in the 90th minute and he was really playing well. Referees still seem to have a thing about this club and if that is a three-match suspension then his loan period is over. Preston Edwards and Tom Kilby (one of the kids Pompey was after) made their debuts. Now that is how to keep them here.

* * *

7 September 2007, Brighton and Hove Albion 3 – 0 Millwall
Here we go again. Lost 3-0 at Brighton and this time Whitbread is sent off in the 90th minute. The penalty that got them on their way was a disgrace and we should have had at least one if not two but there we go, same old story. We need our strikers to score quickly as we're dropping down the table too quickly and that good start will have been wasted.

Looks like Sam Walker (the other kid Pompey wanted) won't be going there after all, he's gone to Chelsea. Still at least we get £500,000 for him, sounded like he would be a good goalkeeper too. Oh well.

We've looked at three more players on trial but none will get a contract as Donachie says they won't add anything to the squad. Somebody who can score better get here and do it pretty soon.

There are rumours that Daniel Sturridge or Dean Bowditch could be on their way to us on loan. Well whatever happens we need somebody to put the ball in the net and we need him fast.

* * *

15 September 2007, Millwall 1 – 2 Walsall

Still no striker has scored. This time it was Frampton but again we lost 1-2 because of poor defending. Walsall did not play all that well and we should have been able to beat them, but once again we could not put our chances away.

At least we seem to have sorted out the goalkeeping problem bringing Rab Douglas in on loan from Leicester. I think Edwards would have been between the sticks if he hadn't got injured but Douglas is only here for one month so we'll wait and see.

There's no conviction in our play and only Leeds and Oldham are below us now, and remember Leeds started the season with minus fifteen points. Things are not looking good.

O'Hara has signed for another two months on loan. I like him and I think he could do well for us. We've also signed a striker, Will Hoskins, on a one-month loan from Watford. Donachie likens him to Kenny Dalglish so that's probably the end of his goal-scoring career.

We are also supposed to be after Dwayne Mattis from Barnsley but do we really need yet another midfield player?

* * *

22 September 2007, Crewe Alexandra 0 – 0 Millwall

Well I suppose the 0-0 draw at Crewe was a point gained but we are still third from bottom and we are still struggling to score. Without the point we would be the bottom club. Hoskins made his debut but should have scored very early on. I guess we need to give him time though.

Donachie made four changes to his starting line up so we need to give him credit for trying. The irony is that Byfield, Hubertz and Zebroski (who have left) are all scoring and that hurts, especially as we had twenty-three shots at goal and thirteen corners in the game. Making changes is fine but we really must start taking some of the chances we are creating or we are in big trouble.

I don't understand. We are having trouble scoring and we let Ben May go on a three-month loan to Scunthorpe. Good move for him I suppose going up a division and I know he hasn't been performing well but all the same what is happening here? Even though we have a re-call clause in his loan, I bet we sell him in January.

* * *

29 September 2007, Millwall 1 – 2 Swindon Town

At last a striker scores so well done Jay Simpson, however, we still lost the match 1-2. Swindon really did not deserve all the points, especially after our second half display and Chris Hackett changed the game when he came on, so why not start with him?

Once again we gave away goals that we should have stopped and I do not think Donachie can last much longer. There are rumblings among the fans now and although we have got quite a few injured players, like we did this time last season, could history be about to repeat itself?

OCTOBER

Dwayne Mattis went to Walsall instead of here, which might be the reason they are now off the bottom of the table but we are still supposed to be after another midfield player. This time it is James Ashmore from Sheffield United.

* * *

2 October 2007, Millwall 2 – 0 Northampton Town
A win at last and we were pretty good value for 2-0. Northampton were not up to much though, getting stuck in traffic and having both their central defenders replaced early in the game might have helped us, but a win is a win, and Dunne and Robinson scored good goals.

That might have held off the wolves from Donachie's door for a while but I'm still worried about our strikers not scoring and the result has not helped us in the league table either.

Well Tom Kilby went to Portsmouth after all. Why can't we keep good kids anymore? Maybe we do not want to.

* * *

6 October 2007, Carlisle United 4 – 0 Millwall
Rock bottom! That is where we are after losing 4-0 at Carlisle and all those were scored in the first half. I do not know what is going on here but surely Donachie can't last much longer.

Donachie apologises for Saturday's game, Till says there was no board meeting to discuss the manager and we are after another midfield player in Blackburn's Bryan Hodge. I think anyone who comes here at the moment is either mad or desperate, and what is Donachie's obsession with midfield players?

* * *

Goodbye Willie, you were never going to survive much longer. Shaw and West are looking after the team while a new manager is found, not that bad I suppose but please do not take the easy option this time when appointing a new boss. Shaw does not want it so maybe we will start looking properly right from the start.

* * *

Plenty of names in the frame for the new manager, 'Mad Dog' Allen seems to be who a lot of fans want but I am not sure I'd like him here. I would not mind Micky Adams or Paul Jewell out of the other names on the supposed list but what about Alex Rae?

* * *

13 September 2007, Gillingham 1 – 1 Millwall

Well a points a point and although we are still in the drop zone, we are off the bottom. I suppose a 1-1 draw at Gillingham is not that bad and Dunne can't seem to stop scoring, although it might have gone in without him touching it. If it had, we would have had our second goal from a striker this season.

At least Shaw had the presence of mind to start with Hackett and he proved that was the correct thing to do as he set up so many chances. We have to start taking them soon, although we might not be too far away from seeing that happen.

Pidgeley played in the reserves so at least someone is on their way back. Anyway Douglas did well while he was here so thanks Rab, and the best of luck wherever you go next.

Will Hoskins has agreed to a second month on loan. Wish he would hurry up and start scoring though. Mind you I should say that for almost all the squad.

* * *

20 October 2007, Millwall 2 – 1 Bournemouth

What a list for the manager's job – that have turned it down, not who might take it: Ronnie Moore, Russell Slade, Kenny Jackett and Steve Tilson. The fans favourite is still 'Mad Dog' Allen and he has said he would like it as well but I am not too sure about him.

I can't believe so many fans are wearing pink today for the breast cancer awareness match. You would not have seen that here a few years ago, it shows how much the club has changed and I would say for the better; although I am sure there are many that wouldn't agree with me.

Maybe we should wear pink all the time as we beat Bournemouth 2-1 and we are out of the bottom four. Hoskins scored at last, although if he had missed that one I think we would all have berated him. Nice goal by O'Hara to open the scoring.

* * *

John Berylson has taken over as chairman of the football club now with Stewart Till going to Vice Chairman. Till says this is because of work commitments.

Typical of this club though is the injury problems we have. Hackett gets back into the first team and then does his knee, and Dave Brammer is injured as well. It sounds like they both need operations and with the others that are out it does not look good.

* * *

Now there is talk of Gordon 'Merlin' Hill as manager. I know 'Merlin' has been coaching for a long time but can he manage or is there some sort of American connection coming to the fore.

Willie Donachie must have known something about us needing midfield players, which was why he was always trying to bring some more into the club. Now with so many out we have brought in Ahmet Brkovic on loan from Luton until the beginning of December. Their fans call him 'The Croatian Sensation', so I hope he can do something for us.

* * *

27 October 2007, Leeds United 4 – 2 Millwall

Did not expect to take any points from Leeds although I hoped we could, and maybe we would have but for some silly defending again. Pidgeley really must learn to kick. Three goals in five minutes are too many to give away for any side. Still it was good to see we tried to come back from four down and with Hoskins scoring again and Brkovic scoring on his debut maybe things will get better.

I suppose the game away at Altringham in the FA Cup is a potential banana skin but there is no reason why we should not get through to the next round, is there?

Physio Terry Standring has gone, probably because there were too many to cope with on the treatment table. I make it eleven now and counting. Hope the new man, Graham McAnuff, can get some back as soon as possible.

NOVEMBER

Now Mick Harford has gone from QPR he has been added to the list of potential managers. Others include Kit Symons, Leroy Rosenior and Scott Fitzgerald. I wish the board would sort this saga out soon as it can't be good for the players and it certainly is not for the fans.

We have signed another midfield player on loan. This time it is Bryan Hodge from Blackburn and we have recalled Ben May form Scunthorpe. This injury problem is getting worse by the day.

* * *

3 November 2007, Millwall 0 – 1 Hartlepool United

Hodge made his debut against Hartlepool and May played as a substitute but we still lost 0-1. Hartlepool did not play that well but we look a shambles. Only O'Hara, Alexander, Brkovic and Senda look like they want to play. We need a manager fast.

Mike Newall and Peter Grant are in the frame for the manager's position now but we have tried again for Russell Slade. Oh well!

* * *

6 November 2007, Millwall 2 – 2 Swansea City

Drew 2-2 with Swansea and they only had two shots on goal. Whitbread took his goal well after he replaced Shaw, and Dunne blasted the penalty home. Glad he had the confidence to do it. However, more players join the injury list with Senda, Harris, May and Shaw fighting for places on the treatment table. It is becoming so bad that we have recalled Ross Gaynor from his loan at Fisher.

Still there is some good news at last. Kenny Jackett was named as the new manager just before the game. Hope this will start a turnaround in the club's fortunes.

* * *

Kenny Jackett
with assistant
manager Joe
Gallen.
(*Brian Tonks*)

10 November 2007, English FA Cup, Altrincham 1 – 2 Millwall

I was wrong, Frampton has been added to the injury list now. It seems he played with a broken toe on Tuesday night. We have a whole team out now but at least Jackett is using his contacts as he has brought in Marcus Bignot on loan from QPR. However, we have taken three youth players to Altrincham, which shows how depleted the squad now is.

Well we made it to the next round, but only just. Hoskins was back after injury and scored one of our two goals and Dunne put away another penalty, which saw one of their players sent off but it was really close, especially as we were a goal behind. I thought that Bignot played well on his debut but I really feel sorry for Gary Alexander. He has no luck in front of goal at the moment. The handball on the line was his shot. Can't wait to see what he does when he finally scores.

We have drawn Barrow or Bournemouth at home in the next round. Naturally I hope it is Barrow but I do not expect it will be.

Jackett's brought in another player from his list of contacts – Adebayo Akinfenwa, who is a striker. Can't say I have heard of him and he has been out since breaking his leg last February but Jackett has worked with him at both Watford and Swansea so he must think he is worth having, although he has only on a month-by-month contract.

* * *

17 November 2007, Bristol Rovers 2 – 1 Millwall

Will our luck ever change? Dunne is injured within five minutes and although his replacement Ali Fuseini scored a great goal we still lost 2-1. A penalty that never was and a goal in the 94th minute saw Bristol Rovers get their first home win of the season. Akinfenwa came on as a late sub for his debut when Brkovic was injured and I will leave judgement on him for another time, but more injuries as Bakayoko was struggling at the end as well.

Welcome back Tony Roberts as goalkeeping coach. I liked him as a goalkeeper even though he did not manage to play many games for us before injury took him out of the game. I hope he helps our goalkeepers to improve.

* * *

24 November 2007, Millwall 2 – 1 Yeovil Town

Goodbye Jamie O'Hara. I would like to see you come back from Spurs in January but I bet it does not happen. What a great goal he scored for the equaliser and Fuseini's winner was even better. Shame Hodge only hit the bar or that would have been the best.

Not much of a first half and Yeovil did not look much better, and we are still giving away soft goals but a 2-1 win must lift the players confidence, especially as it took us out of the bottom four.

I was surprised to see Brammer and Harris on the bench. Is this the start of us getting some of our injured players back to fitness? I hope so because some of our other loan players go back soon.

We are supposed to be giving a trial to Brent Sancho but I am not sure if we want a thirty-year-old central defender who can't get into the Gillingham side and has not played for a year. Mind you we are short on central defenders so maybe a short-term contract would be all right if he passes the trial.

Glad to see Brkovic has extended his loan to January. This is a player I would not mind having here on a permanent basis.

DECEMBER

1 December 2007, English FA Cup, Millwall 2 – 1 Bournemouth

Now I am glad Brkovic signed as he made one goal for Hoskins and scored the other in the 2-1 FA Cup win over Bournemouth, and although the first half was rather dire the second half was much better. It was also good to see Ross Gaynor make his debut. I think with the right coaching he could make it. I wonder who we will get in tomorrow's draw.

* * *

4 December 2007, Leyton Orient 0 – 1 Millwall

We got Northampton or Walsall away in the next round. I don't really want to face Northampton again but Walsall are doing well at the moment, so either one will be difficult.

Good win at Leyton Orient and a good goal by Whitbread. He has really come back well this season. We have not moved up the table but the gap is closing and we signed Sancho this afternoon so I hope Jackett has not made a mistake with all these old players he once knew.

Why did they call the match at Luton off so late? Some fans were even in the stadium. Shame really because I thought we had a good chance of winning there. Mind you they are playing Nottingham Forest in the FA Cup on Tuesday so I wonder if that had anything to do with it.

The A.G.M. is tomorrow and Berylson seems a bit worried what Graham Lacey will do. I guess we will see tomorrow.

* * *

15 December 2007, Millwall 2 – 3 Oldham Athletic

Lacey did not agree with the new share option, what is he up to? Maybe he needs watching but I do not think it will be a problem for the club in the long run, at least I hope not.

There was only one reason why we lost 2-3 against Oldham and that sits squarely on the shoulders of the referee. Sending Simpson off after he scored was a disgrace. I know he had already been booked but he was just celebrating with the fans. Referees must start using some discretion. Maybe we should have held on after Whitbread put us in front but the referee was never going to allow us to win the game.

His penalty decision was wrong and why he never even spoke to Lee Hughes for his goal celebrations will remain a mystery. I know he sent one of their players off as well but that was right at the end when the damage was irreparable.

I thought the referee had to stay on the pitch until all the players had left as well, so why did he run straight off at the final whistle? The man nearly caused a riot. Not a good way to celebrate Kitchener's sixtieth birthday.

Harris and Brkovic are both out injured now and that was also Hoskin's last game. I do not want him back; he is not a team player at all. Somebody not coming back is Jamie O'Hara as he is playing in Spurs first team now. See what playing for us can do for you.

* * *

22 December 2007, Millwall 0 – 3 Walsall

Harris is back from injury and scores. Shame it was the last in Walsall's 3-0 win and we have got to go back there to play them in the cup. We will have to do better than that.

* * *

26 December 2007, Millwall 3 – 0 Brighton and Hove Albion

Well now I can say, 'I was there when Gary Alexander scored,' and not once, not twice but three times and the team were good value for the 3-0 win. Brighton were never in the game, although there were still a lot of 'moaning minnies' in the ground. That was our first penalty of the season as well, so more of the same on Saturday against Crewe please.

* * *

29 December 2007, Millwall 2 – 0 Crewe Alexandra

Well it was a win and we did get another penalty. Harris took the penalty well and what a goal by Brkovic. Glad to see him back from injury. Still we lost Alexander early on with a broken nose and Harris went off injured before the end. It seems we get one back and lose two, and the loan players will start to go back soon. What will we do then?

JANUARY

1 January 2008, Northampton Town 1 – 1 Millwall

The year has started well enough I suppose with a 1-1 draw at Northampton, the problem is that Harris got sent off for a fight with Hubertz. He does not score but still makes problems for us. At least Alexander came off the bench to equalise even with his dodgy nose and Jay Simpson is staying for the rest of the season.

It is rumoured that we are after Adrian Forbes from Blackpool and another old player of Jackett's when he was at Swansea. I am not sure if we need another winger but he comes on a free and he can play as a striker and with Hodge, Brkovic and Bignot all ending their loans spells soon it might not be a bad thing.

Jackett says he will be trying to get them all back and also O'Hara, although I can't see that one happening, but at least there is no mention of Hoskins, which I think is a good thing.

* * *

5 January 2008, English FA Cup, Walsall 0 – 0 Millwall

Well we signed Forbes and let Peter Vincenti go to Stevenage. Never saw him play so can't really comment on him.

Two more back from the injury list as May and Frampton played at Walsall and Forbes made his debut. A 0-0 draw was a much better display than the last time we were here so perhaps we can go one better in the replay. Maybe Monday's draw for the next round will help inspire us, especially as the big boys come in now.

I cannot believe Coventry beat Blackburn at Ewood Park and it is them we drew in the next round, quite an incentive to win the replay. We are also supposed to be after another Jackett old boy, this time it is Marc Laird, a midfield player from Manchester City. Well I suppose if you know a player's pedigree it is better than just taking a chance. That is probably Hodge gone though.

* * *

Well I was right and wrong. We tried to get Hodge on a permanent deal but Blackburn wanted money, so that is off. Glad they got knocked out of the cup now. Mind you the same will probably be true for Brkovic and Bignot. Surprised that May turned down a move to Shrewsbury as I thought the 'boo boys' were getting on his back. I am not surprised that Sancho and Akinfenwa have gone though.

Laird signed today and so did Brkovic, and with others starting to come back from injury things might start to look up.

* * *

12 January 2008, Port Vale 3 – 1 Millwall

Should have said 'look down' after this result. Got off to a flyer when Alexander scored and even though they equalised, I thought we were still in the game. Then Shaw gets sent off and we are out of the game. I do not think Port Vale were good 3-1 winners but we were at their place so what should you expect?

Not bad debuts from Laird and Bowes but we will have to wait and see, they both did not have that much time to impress.

* * *

15 January 2008, English FA Cup, Millwall 2 – 1 Walsall

We made hard work off winning the replay and their goal was fluky but May took his well and he set up Alexander's nicely so maybe that will help him. Bignot signing on a free is good news, although Whitbread injuring his toe is typical of our luck at the moment.

It sounds like we are after Dave Martin from Crystal Palace. Why are we really going all out for wingers and would he make it here with a Palace background?

* * *

19 January 2008, Millwall 0 – 1 Tranmere Rovers

I am shocked at May going to Scunthorpe after what he and Jackett said after Tuesday night but on the other hand I am not surprised. He never really fulfilled his potential. Now we are short of strikers so maybe that is why Gavin Grant is back from Grays.

Started the game back in the bottom four after Cheltenham won last night and stayed there after losing 0-1 to Tranmere. We did not deserve that but we made enough chances to win and did not take them but their goal came from yet another poor refereeing decision.

Adrian Forbes covered every blade of grass and looks like a good signing. He was outstanding and unlucky not to have scored a couple of times.

Just seen Akinfenwa has signed for Northampton so that should be interesting to look out for.

* * *

23 January 2008, Millwall 2 – 2 Nottingham Forest

So Grant was not the answer as we have signed a striker from Crystal Palace. Never heard of Lewis Grabban but Neil Warnock thought he had something about him or was that just a ploy to get us to take him.

Has Kenny Jackett got shares in Blackpool? He has now brought in a goalkeeper from there, Rhys Evans, and again we paid nothing for him. Apparently he used to be Pidgeley's understudy at Chelsea.

What a free kick from Harris to score his 100th league goal and Simpson's was a cracker as well, so why did we sit back when we had Forest for the taking. We gave away two silly goals and threw away two points. Maybe it was bringing Dunne on as they scored their first right after that, still I suppose it is another player back from injury. The one point got us out of the bottom four though, so now the game at Cheltenham is more than important.

Evans looks good but not sure about Grabban. He looks a bit raw, we have some work to do on him. Bet that is the end of Pidgeley though, as he was not even on the bench.

* * *

Told you about Pidgeley, Jackett has told him he can go.

We are back in the bottom four again as Cheltenham won last night, still we will have a few games in hand, although I would much prefer the points.

* * *

26 January 2008, English FA Cup, Coventry City 2 – 1 Millwall

That is three games in a row we have dominated and not got our just rewards. Good goal from Simpson but the referee was poor in the decisions that gave Coventry their two goals, and we should have had a penalty. Still there is nothing to distract us now, so we can concentrate on improving our league position.

Keep hearing we are still after Dave Martin and we have got Fisher striker Jeff Goulding on trial. Will we make another mistake like we did with Scannell and not take him on.

* * *

29 January 2008, Cheltenham Town 0 – 1 Millwall

What a win. Okay, it was only 1-0 but Alexander's goal was enough to get us out of the drop zone again. Good to see Bignot and Brkovic back but now Brammer is out for at least a month, and I think we will miss him no matter what the idiots around me say.

Last day of the transfer window and Dave Martin arrives. Will he start on Saturday I wonder?

The South Wales police must have it in for us as they have changed the game at Swansea to a Friday night – AGAIN!

Just seen Dave Livermore has gone to Oldham and we play them in March. Will it happen yet again?

FEBRUARY

2 February 2008, Millwall 0 – 3 Doncaster Rovers

I think Dave Martin must be wondering what he has let himself in for and not playing was probably the best thing for him. Doncaster were amazing. I do not think we were as bad as it seems, they were just that good and 0-3 probably does them an injustice.

The problem now is Evans has joined our injury list so maybe it was a good thing that Pidgeley has not gone, especially as Day is out for the rest of the season. It would have left us with only Edwards if Evans cannot shake his injury off and the other youngsters of course, although I suppose we could get an emergency loan player back in.

* * *

What is going on with Crystal Palace and us? I read in the paper today that we have signed Scott Flinders until the end of the season. I know I said that we might need to get in another goalkeeper on loan because of the injury to Evans, but I can't see anything about it on the club website so I will just have to wait and see.

Here we go again; Will Hoskins has gone to Nottingham Forest until the end of the season and who do we play on Saturday, yes that is right. I know I did not rate him much but just watch the curse of the ex-player strike again.

Kenny Jackett says he is not interested in sorting out contracts for players who have theirs coming to an end this summer just yet. I think that means a few will be on their way out. I am going to guess that will be the following: Lenny Pidgeley, Neil Harris, Chris Day, Zoom Bakayogo, Richard Shaw, Mark Phillips and Ross Gaynor.

I would like to see Harris and Shaw stay if only in a coaching capacity and of course we will probably not keep the players that are out on long term loans, Zebroski and Morais, but we will just have to wait and see.

* * *

9 February 2008, Nottingham Forest 2 – 0 Millwall

Well we are ten points better off overnight now that Bournemouth has gone into administration. I know that is not the best of things to happen but I suppose we will take the points difference wherever they come from.

I just knew we would lose at Forest, but at least Hoskins did not score. Mind you they were two poor goals to give away and it puts us back into the bottom four. Good to see Evans, Whitbread and Bignot back in the side and Martin made his debut when he came on as a substitute for Neil Harris.

Isn't it strange though that we got rid of Akinfenwa and now he has scored two in two for Northampton? We just can't seem to get anything right at the moment. There was no truth in the story about Scott Flinders, although Palace have said he can go so look out for him turning up at the start of next season.

Good to see Jamie O'Hara made the England under-21 team, and nice of him to say it is all down to the coaching he received here. We really could do with his enthusiastic play at the moment.

* * *

12 February 2008, Millwall 2 – 1 Southend United

We can come back from being a goal behind. I did not think we would pick ourselves up after we went behind so early but we did and all credit to everyone in doing so. There was a well-taken goal from Alexander and a great free kick from Martin. Hope his injury does not put him on to our injury list now because I thought he played well.

I know they had a player sent off but I do not think that affected the result as there was only 10 minutes left and we are back out of the bottom four again.

* * *

I should have kept my mouth shut as Martin is out for a while. Strange about Gavin Grant though. I thought he was brought back to play some part in the squad but he has gone out on loan again, this time to Stevenage for a month.

The referees reported the incident on Tuesday night, which was for somebody throwing something. What a time to do it with the club meeting the FA next week. We could be in big trouble now. When will these so called supporters realise that all they do is drag the club down. They are not supporters at all in my opinion, just brainless thugs.

* * *

16 February 2008, Tranmere Rovers 2 – 0 Millwall

Well we are still out of the bottom four even though we lost to Tranmere. Another two poor goals to give away, and two more scored by Zebroski and Akinfenwa for their respected clubs. We could do with that at the moment.

* * *

19 February 2008, Huddersfield 1 – 0 Millwall

It looked like a dodgy penalty to me but it is three points gone begging again. I thought we would at least get a point at Huddersfield as well.

Amazing! It seems like the FA have been a bit lenient as I thought we might have had points taken off of us. However, the club have said that only season ticket holders will be able to sit in the lower West Stand, where the trouble came from last Tuesday and I hope that is it. Any more problems and I can see all sorts of things happening, including ID cards, member only games again or even matches played behind closed doors. When will these fools ever learn?

Good to see Ryan Smith and Tom Brighton get a run out in the reserves. Both have been out for some time now and who knows, that might be the start of getting them back into the team and us getting out of relegation trouble.

* * *

23 February 2008, Millwall 3 – 0 Port Vale

Were we that good or were Port Vale that bad? I would like to think the former and the goals from Grabban, Laird and especially Martin were brilliant. We should have had at least three more and could have had another three as well. Ryan Smith was on the bench and I hoped he would get at least a run out but it did not happen, still there is time. What a great way to celebrate Dockers Day, especially as some of the team that had the fifty-nine unbeaten home match record were there.

We signed Baz Savage last night until the end of the season. I wonder if he was watching the game. I suspect that really does mean the end for Harris because Jackett would not have brought in another striker if he were going to take some part in the final run in. Shame really because he will never get the chance to get those elusive six goals he needs for the record.

* * *

26 February 2008, Luton Town 1 – 1 Millwall

I was right about Harris, Jacket has told him he will not get a new contract at the end of this season and he will help him find a club on loan if he wants to take that route. I was pleased to hear him say he will stay and fight for a spot.

We could have done with his goals having drawn 1-1 at Luton. Savage made his debut and I suppose he might have something to add to the squad and perhaps Grabban's goal will help, as a point is not too bad a result but we really need to start winning games.

Who though, was the idiot that threw the flare onto the pitch? Wish I knew as I would not wait a second in letting the authorities know if I did.

We are giving a trial to Kevin Nowland. Jackett must have a list of players who are not contracted to anyone and if he knows them from somewhere just brings them in. I am not sure if that is a good thing or not, it has a Dennis Wise 'jobs for the boys' smell about it, although I hope I am wrong.

The financial report for the club says we are still losing loads of money but are 22 per cent better off than this time last season. Well I suppose that is something.

It was good to hear that some fans have named the flare thrower. I hope that is the right person and if it is he should never be allowed in any Millwall game again as far as I am concerned. He is certainly no fan of the club.

MARCH

1 March 2008, Millwall 0 – 1 Bristol Rovers

What is it with 90th minute goals against us? I would have been happy with a 0-0 against Bristol Rovers and then we give away another silly late goal and lose the game. I am sure Alexander's disallowed goal was a good one as well, which makes it hurt even more.

Good to see Ryan Smith back on the pitch but Grabban and Savage have joined the injury list now. Will that ever stop? I am glad that Peter Garston has been re-elected as the 'Fan on the Board' and unopposed as well. I think he did a good job before so he can continue now where he left off.

* * *

More injury news and this time it is about Danny Spiller. Seems he needs another operation. Maybe he is going to be another Tom Brighton, but it was good to hear he has played another reserve game. You never know we might actually see him play this season.

Kenny Jackett has said he wants to keep Jay Simpson. Well I suppose that depends on what money they want for him and what division we are playing in next season. I can't see him getting into Arsenal's first team but you never know where he could end up next season, although I would like to see him stay.

* * *

7 March 2008, Swansea City 1 – 2 Millwall

I don't believe it. Going to Swansea and hoping for a draw was beyond my wildest dreams, to come home 1-2 winners was great. Grabban's first minute goal really shook them up and then Simpson putting us further in front really did it for us.

And what an important three points it turned out to be with the results at other games going our way on Saturday. Three more points closer to safety and a point at Yeovil on Tuesday will help as well.

I can't wait for this season to be over. Not because of our up and down league position, as worrying as that is, but because of the injuries we keep getting. I know all clubs get them but now we have added Forbes to the list and he will be out for several weeks. Furthermore, Brkovic, Bignot, Grabban and Alexander are all carrying bad knocks that we could do without.

* * *

11 March 2008, Yeovil Town 0 – 1 Millwall

Another three points! Wake me up I am dreaming. I never expected to win at Yeovil but Savage's goal was enough to do it. The win came at a price though with Alexander being out for a while. Thanks Marvin. That was a bad tackle that took him out. Still if we keep playing like this who knows, we might even make the play-offs (haha).

We are now giving a trial to another midfield player in Justin Cochrane. I guess we need to look to the future and it is probably better to do that now rather than later.

***

15 March 2008, Millwall 0 – 1 Leyton Orient

Two steps forward and a million back. Thanks Andy D'Urso, you made some controversial decisions against us and your assistants were no better either. I am sure the reason Orient scored was because our players had been frightened off from making tackles. Laird's sending off looked to me like two players going for the ball fairly and we should have had at least three penalties. In fact, we should have had two for the last incident in the box alone.

Isn't it strange how officials can't see blatant penalties but can see a tackle worthy of a red card?

Our problem now will be about the fool who threw the bottle onto the pitch. I can understand the frustration with referees and assistants when they are like that but it is got to be a bit worrying as D'Urso's match report is bound to mention it as being thrown at his assistant. With the problems already standing over us who knows what that might mean.

Harris lifted the crowd when he came on, although it was perhaps too little too late for him to do much. All these injuries are now having a big effect on us. We can mix and match with the strikers but Ali Fusini is now our only fit central midfield player now that Laird has got a three-match ban.

***

Well there is the answer; we have signed Cochrane until the end of the season and also another midfield player on loan, Jem Karacan from Reading for a month.

I am surprised Richard Shaw has been told he will get another contract, even though it is a player/coach role. Maybe he will become the assistant manager now that West is going and maybe that is a route Harris can take and become our striker's coach.

***

22 March 2008, Oldham Athletic 1 – 1 Millwall

Why do old players come back to haunt you. I thought that Savage's goal at Oldham would be enough to get us all three points but Constantine's equaliser made it only one. I suppose it could have been worse and David Livermore could have scored as well. At least we are still out of the bottom four but things are getting tight. We need to get another couple of wins very soon to ease the tension.

Karacan looked like he could do us a job but I will hold judgement on Cochrane until I get to see more of him.

* * *

24 March 2008, Millwall 0 – 0 Luton Town

Three points should have come against Luton and a 0-0 draw has not helped at all, a very boring first half and a not much better second. How did Brkovic hit the bar rather than score? Mind you Savage missed from an inch away. Why was Harris not even on the bench? I can't believe he would have missed that one.

Now we know the reason for Shaw's contract. He is taking over as reserve team manager and Joe Gallen has been promoted to Jackett's assistant. Now that really does smack as jobs for the boys so I hope he is as good as Jackett thinks he is.

* * *

29 March 2008, Bournemouth 2 – 0 Millwall

What a surprise signing Tony Craig on loan until the end of the season and we do need somebody with all these injuries we have. Shame he could not help us in the loss at Bournemouth.

I am sure if Harris had scored from the penalty we would have won instead of having lost 2-0 but then again Brkovic should have put the rebound away and he missed a real sitter as well. It is these misses that could be costly come the end of the season and things are really getting tight now. Saturday's match against Gillingham has really become more of a must win game than it should be.

Just seen that Leeds have sold all their allocation of tickets for their match here and we have taken the rest off general sale. Seems like a sensible move to me, we really do not want any more trouble in the ground.

APRIL

Oh no! Gillingham won last night so the game against them on Saturday really does take on a special meaning.

Seems like Arsenal have said we can have Jay Simpson next season. If they want money for him I hope it will not be too much but the trouble is that it will alert other clubs, and I am sure that somebody else will come sniffing if we do not move to sort him out a contract pretty quickly after the season ends.

The administration rumours are doing the rounds again and it is good to see John Berylson has enough faith in the club to put in another £3 million. That should help a lot.

* * *

5 April 2008, Millwall 1 – 1 Gillingham

A 1-1 draw with Gillingham and I hope that will be enough. We really did slaughter them but as usual we could not put the ball in the net. Robinson's goal was one that any striker would be proud of and there is no doubt that he is my player of the season.

The gap is closing up all over the place and although we are still in nineteenth place in the table, anything can still happen.

Graham Lacey is back in the news again. Just what is he up to? Maybe he really is after everything and that could well mean the end of the club or another move. We really must sort this guy out as soon as possible. How can we get his shares off him? Maybe that is what he wants.

* * *

12 April 2008, Hartlepool United 0 – 1 Millwall

A great win at Hartlepool and Simpson took the goal well, although once again we should have scored more. Still, other results were good for us as well and we have moved a couple of places up the table. I still think we only need another two points to be safe, so let's get them against Leeds.

Anyway let's say goodbye to Luton and Port Vale as they have both been relegated and I hope Swansea do not give up playing now that they have been promoted. That won't do us any good at all. I still think that the Gills will go but look out for Bournemouth, they could be the sting in the tale.

The Leeds case for the return of their fifteen point deduction starts tomorrow and I am glad Millwall have asked for the result not to be announced before our match with them in case it causes trouble. I do not think they should get them back after the way they used the system at the end of last season. Anyway, did not the FA set a precedent with the Hammers last season when they said they could not deduct points from them because it would change too many things? This is exactly the same in reverse.

Things have gone our way a bit now that Jem Karacan can stay until the end of the season. I like the way he plays and he will be quite an asset to us. Shame we won't be able to get him next season. Talking of next season, it seems that Kenny Jackett has decided who will stay or go. Well we know Harris is one but it will be interesting to see how the prediction I made in February turns out.

* * *

19 April 2008, Millwall 0 – 2 Leeds United

Dominated another game and still lost. There is no way that Leeds were two goals better than us. We would have walked it if Karacan's shot had gone in instead of hitting the bar. Mind you we still have trouble putting the ball in the net and they showed how it is done, twice. It is heartbreaking.

Bournemouth won again and so did Crewe and thankfully Bristol Rovers got a late equaliser or Gillingham would have done as well. Now it is any five for the last two relegation places. We really must win against Carlisle now; I do not fancy a last game of the season win to keep us safe.

Another short-term player gone, this time Justine Cochran. I am all in favour of not keeping players who do not fit in but we seem to have done this a lot with Kenny Jacket so far this season. Maybe we need to get the scouting right first time.

Who is Chris O'Grady? I know we want a striker but if he does not want to come, and he cannot play until next season anyway, then we should not chase after him now. It will be his loss. Perhaps he does not want to move far away from Rotherham.

Well done Paul Robinson in winning the player of the year award. It has not been a good season for us but he has had an outstanding one. Let's move forward now, starting on Saturday, and get the bit between our teeth for next season.

* * *

26 April 2008, Millwall 3 – 0 Carlisle United

Were Carlisle really in the second automatic promotion spot before we played them? Any stranger at the game would think it was us instead. We were brilliant. Having a player sent off for the tackle on Harris did not really make a difference as they were well beaten anyway and well done to him for scoring one and making the other two for Simpson and Craig. I know he is not the same and we do need another striker but I got all choked up at the end, sentimental old me. Goodbye Neil, we will miss you but you played your part in making us safe today.

That is a nice touch from Berylson to pay half the cost of the coach fare to Swindon. Let's hope we go out with a bang and get the win that gestures like this deserve.

Oh Palace, fancy recalling Tony Craig just before our last game of the season. I suppose they have to do what they think is right for them. So he said goodbye to the fans with a goal as well. It would be nice if he came back for next season though.

What a surprise that Danny Spiller played and scored in the reserves. I think it will be too late for him or any of the other long term injured players to make an impression on Kenny Jackett though. He will have to go on what he already knows and what he has been told.

Congratulations to Jay Simpson on winning the PFA Player of the Year for League One. I do not expect we will see him next season but stranger things have happened.

* * *

Leeds did not get their fifteen points back. Good. That is what happens when you try and bend the rules. Hope they do not go up from the play-off games either because I think they might struggle next season.

* * *

3 May 2008, Swindon Town 2 – 1 Millwall

Danny Senda finally scores his first goal for the club and then becomes the first long term injury for next season. A dislocated kneecap must be pretty painful and I wish him all the best as he tries to get himself fit.

We lost the match as well. Their first goal was never a penalty, but what has ever stopped that from happening and a wicked deflection for their winner. Oh well there is always next season.

* * *

Now that was a surprise, I thought Hackett would get a new contract, if for no other reason than maybe not getting Simpson for next season. One for Zebroski was also expected, well a bit, because he can score and we do need a striker. Harris getting one was a shock; especially after the things Jackett said earlier in the season, although lately he has been saying things that I thought showed he might have changed his mind. Goodbye to Day, Brighton (shame we never saw the best of you), Phillips, Grant, Callaghan, Gaynor, James, Evans and Bakayogo. Now it is up to Jackett to get some quality players in. I am looking forward to what happens during this closed season.

CHAPTER FOUR

ALMOST THERE
SEASON 2008/2009

CLOSED SEASON

Not the way a closed season should start, with rumours about the team's captain going. Please Robbo do not go to Ipswich. I know it would be a good move for you but at the same time I do think that this club will do a lot better next season with the right amount of work done on it and the right players coming in. Still the fact that he was player of the year last season puts him in the 'up for a move' department I suppose.

Thanks Oppida for your sponsorship last season and it is good to hear that you are also staying as secondary sponsors for this coming season as well. The big question now is who the main sponsor will be. Whoever it is, I hope they put some money in, as we certainly need it.

There are big rumours about the academy becoming a school of excellence. Apart from who they play against I am not sure what the difference is, but if it saves the club money and still brings some good young players through then I am all for it. Does it really matter what it is called as long as the benefit from it is new young players?

I am right behind Kenny Jackett about the medical staff here. I do not mean that they can't do their jobs but with all the injuries we had last season something needs to be done and I hope it gets sorted out, and we do not have another season like the last one where injuries are concerned. Talking of injuries it is sad to hear that Danny Senda will be out for nine months. We will miss him. I am glad to see that Hackett has been kept on. I know it is only a six month contract, which I suppose is fair considering the injuries he had. I am sure that he can earn a longer one if he is given the chance to show what he can do.

There is plenty of talk about players coming in but it is not talk we want, it is action, so let's see some of it.

* * *

This Graham Lacey problem doesn't seem to want to go away. We need to find out what he is up to and get that sorted out quickly.

Our first new signing and again Jackett goes back to where he knows and gets a youngster from Manchester City. I am not against that as I think he knows what he is doing so Ashley Grimes, let's see if the faith the manager has in you is justified. According to what I have read he can play both up front and midfield. Only by the end of the season will we be able to tell, but if he turns out to be as good as Marc Laird then I won't be complaining.

I have heard that Zebroski is not happy and Harris has not signed his new contract either. What is going on? We know we need strikers so what are we doing to keep the ones we have, if the manager really wants to keep them?

* * *

Tony Burns has come back and signed a new contract, how typical of Millwall to have a good quality goalkeeping coach and no goalkeeper. Okay, we have Pidgely but Jackett wants rid of him and Edwards will be second choice, if that. Please let's get a good one as soon as possible.

So the new shirt sponsors are logistics and distribution company CYC. I cannot say I have ever heard of them but if they are willing to put money into the club that is good enough for me.

At last Harris has signed a one-year contract. I am glad because his love for the club and his enthusiasm and experience will help the younger players no end. I just hope Jackett gives him a chance to prove it was worth it. Come on Neil get those goals that give you the record and us promotion.

Meanwhile, I hope Brammer stays as well, although I know he would prefer to move nearer home. Again his experience will help the younger players in the side and they will need all the help they can get.

* * *

At last a goalkeeper and one we know well, he saved a Harris penalty last season, so welcome David Forde, you now have two years to show us what you can do and have a go at Cardiff at the same time for letting you go. We really do need a commanding goalkeeper so I hope you are it.

Shame about Jeff Burnige standing down from the board but after the death of his wife I suppose it was likely to happen. It is a shame how the club used him in the past though and I hope they do not do that again, although Berylson seems to have the good of the club at heart.

* * *

Now Dunne and Brammer need to have operations to sort out their injury problems. I have got a horrible feeling that neither of them will be fit for the beginning of the season, so that will put us three down before we even start.

Well done Millwall for opening up the West Stand as normal from next season. Now all we need are the individuals who forced its closure not to abuse it and we are moving along the right lines. We are drawn against Northampton in the Carling Cup and it is at home. I would like to get as far as being drawn against one of the big boys. I can't see us getting too far but let's face it, getting out of this division must be our top priority. However, if winning a few cup matches gives us a winning mentality then I am all for it. Roll on Monday and the season fixture list.

* * *

The fixture list looks good. Some good games early in the season that should mark out how our season will go. Let's get a good start and not put relegation pressure on ourselves this time.

Zebroski and Gavin Grant have both gone to Wycombe Wanderers. I hope we do not miss either of them and good luck to them both. However, we still need to bring more players into the club.

I have just read about Tim Carter being found dead in Manchester. I know he was not everyone's favourite and maybe he was not the best we have ever seen here at The Den but the 'Telly Tubby' served us well. It is sad to hear about it.

* * *

Things are going on at board level and Lacey is in the middle of it. First Berylson converts £2.5 million of loans into shares then Peter De Savary does the same with his. I expect Paphitis will have some that he can do the same with as well. All I, and the majority of our fans, want, is for this to get sorted. We do not want the club folding but it looks like this could happen if the bickering over this regeneration thing does not stop.

Now Lacey says he will be happy if Heather Rabbatts goes. Well it looked to me as if she was doing all right so what is he playing at. Hope he gets defeated at the E.G.M.

* * *

I have been reading rumours that McCammon and Byfield want to come back here. Not sure of either of them really. I know we could do with Byfield's goals and maybe McCammon is the big man up front that we miss but I think both of them could be too disruptive and we would therefore be better off without them.

The new kit is out and I like it. Glad we stayed with white for the change strip as well. Not sure about the sponsors logo but if that is how it has to be then so be it.

Well the E.G.M. went the way of the board and I am glad, although it was a close run thing. Maybe we can get on and sort out the team now. It is football that we are here for isn't it?

* * *

Maybe Brammer is on his way as we have signed another midfield player, this time Frenchman Nadjim Adbou, who is known as Jimmy. Got him free from Plymouth and that is probably the way we will have to keep going, picking up free and out-of-contract players for a while.

We are looking at a couple of players on trial on the Irish tour, so we will have to see what comes of those. Meanwhile McCammon's gone to Gillingham and Byfield to Doncaster. So much for them wanting to come here, we just did not want them. Baz Savage has also gone, to Tranmere, and he won't be a big loss to us either (just watch him make me eat those words). We might need to look out for Dave Livermore though now he is at Brighton.

Pidgeley has gone on trial at Motherwell, so we will still need another goalkeeper as Jackett does not want him. I wonder if McGhee will. Welcome home Tony Craig. I did not think we would let you go after your loan spell here at the end of last season. Dave Brammer did not go to Ireland and has been told he can go. Shame really as I think we missed him at the tail end of last season.

* * *

The Irish tour was cut short by one game but we did all right drawing one and winning one, then coming back and drawing with Reading. Good to see Harris scored twice as well.

Another couple of good work out games drawing with Spurs and beating Ebbsfleet and maybe Jackett is getting an idea of his preferred first eleven. Although, with the cup games now having seven substitutes it means eighteen players will be looking to get into his good books by the start of the season.

I have just heard about the death of Nicky Milo, another good servant of the club has gone.

Lost the last pre-season game unless there is another closed door one before the season starts. We still seem a bit short in the strike force area but who knows, the season starting is what matters.

* * *

Transfer deadline day and we have signed Tresor Kandol on loan from Leeds for six months. Well I did say we looked a bit short on the striker front. He scored ten goals last season which was better than our strikers so that is a positive but I will be interested to see what the line up is on Saturday at Oldham.

2008/2009 Millwall squad, at the start of the season. *(Chris Bethell)*

AUGUST

9 August 2008, Oldham Athletic 4 – 3 Millwall

Scoring in the first couple of minutes and away from home is a good way for Kandol to make his debut, and with Grabban getting one and an own goal putting us 1-3 up it looked like a good start. However, nothing has changed from last season with referees.

It was a poor decision to give Oldham a penalty and an even worse one to send off Robinson, and from that moment on I knew it would go from bad to worse but losing 4-3 is a bit irksome. We should know how to hold on when we are winning like that. Forde never really had much of a chance with the goals but that will upset him on his debut and Abdou did not look bad on his either. Hackett played at full back? Well it was just to replace Dunne so maybe that is all right.

I am glad to see that we are appealing against Robbo's red card but I bet the FA say no.

* * *

12 August 2008, English League Cup, Millwall 0 – 1 Northampton

I was right. The FA would not rescind Robbo's red card but I am not sure it would have made much of a difference tonight. We were awful in the first half apart from the last fifteen minutes and although we looked a lot better in the second, we still can't score.

I am not sure if Northampton deserved to win 0-1 and with Grabban hitting the post, and the penalty we did not get when Kandol was pulled down, things could have been different but we still missed plenty of other chances.

So goodbye to the Carling Cup; I thought Hackett looked all right at full back after a shaky start. Has Jackett found something here?

* * *

16 August 2008, Millwall 1 – 1 Southend United

Are we going to struggle this season as well? Brkovic saved our bacon and a 1-1 draw was all we and Southend deserved, although it was a poor attempted catch from Forde that gave them their goal.

We played some good football at times but we did that last season and struggled. Once again there was no end product to our approach play.

Pidgely has gone on loan to Woking but to be honest I am not sure if Forde is any better. Still it is early days I suppose and I will reserve judgement for now.

* * *

23 August 2008, Northampton Town 0 – 0 Millwall

A point away from home is always welcome and Northampton did beat us just a few days ago so perhaps that is some improvement but we still did not score and that must be a worry.

We are in the bottom three again and that has a familiar look about it and so does the side. Jackett must decide what his best starting eleven and formation is, and he must do it quickly.

Four games into the season and we already top the disciplinary table. I really do think that referees have a mental thing about Millwall and that they need to show cards in every game.

Now we have another problem. Why did Fuseini have to double up on agents? Being a Lions player the FA are sure to come down hard on him and I bet this affects his game as well.

Can somebody tell me what Ryan Smith has done to upset Kenny Jackett? We almost let him go to NEC Nijmegen but he is back now. Jackett says he is happy with the squad we have now so I suppose that means we will bring nobody else in before the transfer window closes.

* * *

So much for believing Jackett; he brings in another player from the Manchester City youth team and a left-winger as well. Welcome Karl Moore and does that mean that Smith is now further down the pecking order? I know he is only here on loan until the end of January but like Kandol, if he is good enough he will probably stay. Goodbye Ryan.

* * *

30 August 2008, Millwall 2 – 1 Huddersfield Town

What a great win against Huddersfield. I know it was only 2-1 but it has moved us up to thirteenth in the table and we were a goal down. Kandol and Grabban both took their goals well and what a penalty save by Forde, maybe I am slowly coming round to him.

Shame Harris hit both posts but it is good to see him back in the starting line-up and Moore looked good on his debut as well.

SEPTEMBER

2 September 2008, Johnstone's Paint Trophy, Millwall 0 – 1 Colchester United

What is it about cup competitions? We were back to our old ways against Colchester and we deserved no more than losing 0-1, although being out of the Johnson's Paint Trophy is not the end of the world. It was a disgraceful decision by the referee not to award a penalty when Brkovic was kicked in the head and then he had the nerve to make him leave the pitch to change his shirt because of the blood on it.

Mind you it is typical of our luck that they hit the bar and then the ball hit Forde on the way out and it goes into the net. We hit the underside of the bar and the ball comes out.

Jackett still looks confused about his best formation but if he is experimenting then I hope he sorts it out sooner rather than later as we need to improve on this performance, although I must say that Hackett gets better with each game at full back.

Heather Rabbatts has been named Business Woman of 2008 and also been made a fellow of Goldsmiths College. I know that has nothing to do with football but anything that keeps Millwall's name in the press, as long as it is good, is fine with me.

* * *

6 September 2008, Millwall 2 – 0 Hartlepool United

What a difference confidence makes and that 2-0 win over Hartlepool was full of confidence. Grabban and Alexander both took their goals well but everybody played a part and played it well. The acid test will be at Leicester next Saturday. If we manage to come away losing 1-0 that will be proof of a big improvement to me.

John Berylson says he wants Jackett to stay for the next ten years. Well I do not know about that but he looks like he is building a side and I will give him until the end of next season before judging him.

Looks like we will be saying goodbye to Dave Brammer soon, a shame because I thought he was good for us but I suppose the young kids are making an impact, and as long as they keep learning then it is probably best for him to go.

* * *

13 September 2008, Leicester City 0 – 1 Millwall

What a win. Yes it was only 0-1 but that was three points and Leicester really was a big test, and up to third in the table as well.

Yes I know the other sides have to play yet but who cares. Alexander took his goal brilliantly and gave their defence a lot of problems and so did Kandol. Shame he could not control his temper for just a little while longer, getting sent off in the 90th minute does not help.

Three wins in a row. I can't believe it and am I pushing it to hope for a fourth against Cheltenham next Saturday?

Okay, we dropped down to fifth after all the other games were played but we are still in a play-off position and who would have said that a few weeks ago.

It seems that Everton and Blackburn are looking at Whitbread with a view to buying him in January. There is no doubt in my mind he is a classy player and he will be a good buy for them but I hope it is not goodbye to us as we really do need to keep him.

Chris Hackett in full flight.
(*Brian Tonks*)

I am glad Cheltenham won last night, the first game with a new manager is always a dodgy one for an opposing side and let's face it, Martin Allen is no mug no matter what you think of him. My worry is Barry Hayles. I just wonder what influence he will have on the game.

There is no doubt that Chris Hackett deserves a new contract and I am glad the club is offering him one. It made sense to only give him a short contract after such a long layoff with the knee injury but he has been a revelation at right back and a long contract is a just reward.

* * *

Goodbye to Lenny Pidgely well for a short while anyway. I hope you do well a Woking but it seems that you're off the pitch antics were as much to do with the way the club view you as your poor displays between the posts.

* * *

20 September 2008, Millwall 2 – 0 Cheltenham Town

Barry Hayles certainly had an effect on the game against Cheltenham by getting sent off. I was not too sure at the time but looking at the television replays he certainly head butted Robinson, although I have seen a lot worse just get yellow.

Still the 2-0 win was well deserved and we played some really good football, although I am not sure it was a penalty for Alexander's goal. On the other hand there should have been a couple that were not given and Martin's was a wonder goal. More like that please.

Chris Hackett has signed that new contract and he is ours until 2010 and I am pleased as he is my player of the year so far. I know it is early but he has been brilliant.

* * *

Here we go again. Harris out for six weeks, Kandol suspended for three games, and Alexander had eight stitches in his head in the Cheltenham game. It looks like we are in trouble for strikers on Saturday, so we need something to happen and fast.

* * *

Kenny Jackett must have heard me as he has brought in Jermaine Easter on a month's loan from Plymouth and also Gifton Noel-Williams is training with us and might get a contract as well, so I hope this helps as five wins on the trot after the start we had would be something else.

Easter could have joined us before he went to Plymouth so who knows what will happen now he is here.

* * *

28 September 2008, Swindon Town 1 – 2 Millwall
He played, scored, and got a red card. What is going on with loan players at this club? That is both loan strikers sent off in injury time. If Easter gets a three-match ban we might as well send him back to Plymouth as he won't be much use to us.

Even so we did win at Swindon with Grabban sewing up the points, although I wonder why Whitbread was on the bench. Was something sinister going on?

I thought the club might appeal Easter's red card but they are not, the DVD was not conclusive and I suppose not wanting to take another chance they have accepted the punishment. At least the Whitbread thing was only the fact that he was not feeling well so that solves that mystery.

OCTOBER

Six wins in a row? Who knows but it has got Berylson flying over to watch the game against MK Dons so do not tell me he is not committed to this club as none of us would make an 8,000 mile trip for one game.

The only problem is that Jackett is on the short list for the manager of the month award so I would not buy those tickets just yet in case he wins, as we all know what happens then.

Good and bad news. Noel-Williams signs and is clear to play, Robbie Ryan comes back to the club to coach the under-twelve-year-old side and Kenny Jackett won the kiss of death award. Mind you I seem to remember McGhee or Donachie or even both doing the same, and winning the next game so we will have to wait and see.

Ryan Smith has gone on a three month loan to Southampton and I still cannot understand why he is not in the squad. Chris Hackett revealed that he could have joined two other clubs in a higher league but did not. Now that is loyalty.

* * *

4 October 2008, Milton Keynes Dons 4 – 0 Millwall
Okay, the kiss of death still works with that dreaded trophy although I did not expect losing 4-0. The defending was poor and the last two goals were just a joke. Still Scunthorpe drew and every other side except Leicester at the top of the table lost so it was not as bad as it seems. Mind you we did not play badly but we need to bounce back well at Tranmere.

Noel-Williams played and he looked well out of shape but we do not have any other strikers available to play and he must have been about the only choice that Jackett could have made.

I am glad the club have denied the rumours about moving to the Olympic Stadium in 2012. A lot of fans would not have gone and we would be struggling to find support, especially in West Ham land.

We are supposed to be looking at Tooting winger Michael Antonio but now we have alerted everyone I bet we do not get him.

Hope we do well at Tranmere and that Baz Savage does not upset the apple cart.

* * *

11 October 2008, Tranmere Rovers 1 – 3 Millwall

Well Savage scored but at least it was only a consolation as two goals from a returning Kandol and the first for us from Jimmy Abdou, which Kandol set up, made for a good win.

The problem now is Leeds next week, Kandol can't play in that one and we are short of strikers again. Surely Harris won't be fit enough to play and we have also lost Hackett now, he has been booked again.

More rumours about Whitbread and this time it is West Bromwich that want him. Also it seems that Jackett might be wanted by QPR. Well I suppose when a side are successful then other clubs will look at them, which means we must be doing something right.

Looks like Kandol might stay when his loan ends but who replaces him against Leeds? Hope we get at least a draw.

* * *

18 October 2008, Millwall 3 – 1 Leeds United

It was Harris and what an inspired choice. He made Martin's equalizer and then added two himself, the second was incredible. Welcome back 'Bomber' and now you are only three away from that record.

It will be another hard game on Tuesday night at Colchester but I think we can get something there.

* * *

21 October 2008, Colchester United 1 – 2 Millwall

We are top of the league; say we are top of the league. Well we were until Scunthorpe got a late equaliser. Grabban and Robinson score in a good win at Colchester and we go second on goal difference.

I thought we might struggle there, shows you what I know. Saturday's game against Scunthorpe should be quite something.

So Jermaine Easter wants to stay at The Den for a while. Can't say I blame him. What is better, sitting on the bench at Plymouth going nowhere or being part of a club pushing for promotion?

* * *

25 October 2008, Scunthorpe United 3 – 2 Millwall

You can't give three goals away to the league leaders and hope to win. We did have a good try though and the goals from Harris and Craig nearly got us there, and if Easter's shot had gone in instead of hitting the bar then who knows what would have happened. Harris and Hackett made all the difference when they came on so I hope that is a lesson learned by Jackett.

A potential banana skin with the draw away at Chester in the cup. Still, we should get through.

* * *

28 October 2008, Millwall 1 -0 Hereford United

That was a difficult game against Hereford and Grabban's goal was a welcome relief, poor refereeing though. I do not think either Abdou or Chadwick deserved to be sent off and the conditions did not help. This season has seen some strange and poor refereeing decisions in every division. Still, at least we are second again on goal difference, and we need to do something about that.

Easter gets his wish with his loan extended to Boxing Day. He better pull his finger out because I have not been impressed with him but we need a striker to cover for Alexander who will be out for a while. At least we have a decent replacement in Frampton for Whitbread and he looks like he could be out for some time, although I would prefer him at left back and move Craig into the middle.

NOVEMBER

1 November 2008, Brighton and Hove Albion 4 – 1 Millwall

How did we lose 4-1 at Brighton? Kandol's goal ended up as just a consolation instead of a springboard for a win. We did not play badly but it seemed like they scored every time it looked like we would. What a strange division this is.

Noel-Williams going on loan to Yeovil says it all. He never did look the part but if he gets fit there then who knows? Jackett does make some strange short-term signings but Adam Bolder on loan looks like a good one to me.

What is this about Watford wanting Jackett? I know he was there before but I hope he shows us some loyalty and stays. I like what he is doing here.

* * *

8 November 2008, English FA Cup, Chester City 0 – 3 Millwall

Well we left it late at Chester but the goals from Grabban, Harris and Grimes made sure that banana skin was not trodden on. Hope we see more of

Grimes in the coming months and a good debut from Bolder. Can we get him permanently in January?

Another banana skin draw with either Aldershot or Rotherham. Still at least it is at home.

Here is my opinion on which of the out of contract players should be offered another one: Alexander, Edwards, Frampton, Fuseini, Harris and Spiller. That leaves Barron, Brammer, Brkovic, Forbes, Pidgeley and Smith to go. Dunne I am not sure of either way. Still, what do I know?

* * *

15 November 2008, Millwall 1 – 0 Stockport County

That was a hard win against Stockport. They are the best side I have seen at The Den so far this season. I did not think Martin would hit the target, let alone score with that free kick, so well done.

Mind you the refereeing gets worse. Nine yellow cards in a game that probably needed two at the most but what do you expect from a referee that has given out thirty-nine yellow and four red cards before this game. I counted thirty-nine times he blew his whistle for something in the second half alone.

Pidgeley is back from his loan and they need to get him out again. He is one of the three biggest earners at the club, Brammer and Smith are the other two and they are both on loan as well. That is part of the reason I do not think they will get new contracts.

It is Aldershot and the return of Waddock and Newman. Hope they do not put one over on us.

Just read about last year's loss and £6.1 million is a lot of money for a club our size. It is even bigger than last year and we were supposed to be making savings but I think the E.G.M. did not help. Lacey has a lot to answer for. At least Berylson still seems committed to the club and with the side doing well it might not be so bad next year, although we need more of the missing fans to come back and watch them.

The regeneration plans are in the news again and the club have said that the fans will get a say in the way the stadium looks. I am not too sure about that but it will be interesting after it is finished.

I am not surprised about Easter going, I wish him well at Colchester, although he did nothing for us really except add another red card to our list. However, I am not sure what happened to the Edwards' loan to Woking. Maybe Jackett realised that he would have to use Pidgely in an emergency and so kept him here.

* * *

22 November 2008, Leyton Orient 0 – 0 Millwall

0-0 at Orient and Bignot injured in his first game back, maybe we have picked up another injury prone player. Robinson hit the post but overall it was a boring match. Still it is another point towards promotion and we might be glad of it at the end of the season.

By the way, what a difference in referees, a local derby and only two yellow cards – and neither of them for us.

I said Berylson was committed didn't I? His company have just put another £3.5 million into the club. Hope he takes it back in shares like last time.

* * *

25 November 2008, Millwall 1 – 0 Carlisle United

Wow! How much later can you leave a winning goal? Kandol knocked out Harris in the scramble to get something on the ball. I know Grabban hit a post and that would have made the game easier but we are still missing good opportunities. I counted five for Alexander alone. Still he does work hard so I hope they will come eventually.

What interesting news about Kandol. It seems that Leeds can't take him back until his loan finishes at the end of January unless they are going to sell him. Hope that is true, although if they recall him then his first game will be against us.

* * *

29 November 2008, English FA Cup, Millwall 3 – 0 Aldershot Town

Told you the goals would come for Alexander, two in fact and although he should have had a hat-trick I think he got over excited. Grimes took his goal well too. I think he will be a good player as he develops.

Aldershot played well though, made it hard for us and could have scored a couple themselves. Still we are through to the next round and the big boys come in now, so who is next?

* * *

It is Carlisle or Crewe next in the cup, and a chance to get through to round four. Mind you, we have just played Carlisle, and Crewe will be at The Den only a couple of games before it as well. I do not like that sort of situation.

DECEMBER

Looks like we have got another Tom Brighton in, Danny Spiller and I hope the operation finally sorts things out for him but if he is going to be injury prone then maybe we would be better off letting him go in the summer and we have some good midfield players now, especially if we get Bolder for good.

At least he is staying for another month and if we can get him permanently in January then all the better.

* * *

6 December 2008, Millwall 3 – 2 Bristol Rovers

Bristol Rovers gave us a fright. Still, winning 3-2 is still winning. That last ten minutes was a heart-in-the-mouth moment. Kandol took both his goals well and Alexander's was a contender for the goal of the season. Can anyone tell me what the red card was all about?

Well now we know. It seems the referee thought he had booked Abdou twice when in fact it was Kandol. Says a lot about the kind of referees we get here. First it takes him a couple of minutes to think about sending him off and he can't tell the difference between a 6 ft plus lump and a much smaller twig. Anyway, I thought referees were supposed to write down the name and number of players shown cards.

I am not surprised the club have extended Noel-Williams' loan at Yeovil. At least he can't play against us and the inevitable happen. If we do lose Kandol at least Noel-Williams might be fit by then to be in contention for a place, although I think his contract ends about then as well so he will probably go.

Kenny Jackett wants to keep Karl Moore until the end of the season. I must admit I like him although he needs to put on a bit more muscle. Dave Martin's form has limited his chances as well, although maybe him being here has helped bring Martin on.

* * *

13 December 2008, Walsall 1 – 2 Millwall

At last! Harris gets the record equalling goal. Shame it was away from home but he can now establish the record as his own at the next home game. It must have been playing on his mind but it is always the same for anybody. You just need one more something and it is always hard to find.

I am glad that Frampton scored the winner as well. He has been playing really well and came close to scoring a few times recently. A 1-2 win at Walsall is a good victory as they are not easy to beat, especially at home. The confidence of the squad must grow by the day. Can we really be wishing for promotion? I hope we do not blow it now.

What a shame about Danny Senda. What he did not need was another operation on his knee so I guess that is him out for the rest of the season. Hope he comes back strong for the next one, as I really like him as a player.

* * *

20 December 2008, Millwall 0 – 0 Crewe Alexandra

We really have to beat the teams at the bottom of the league table and getting a 0-0 home draw with Crewe is not really good enough. I know we might look back at the end of the season and say what a good point that was but it really should have been three.

There was a lot of huff and puff but no real end product. It was as if we had mentally switched off for lots of the game. I bet the cup game will be different.

There are rumours that Jamie Shawcroft will be joining us from Crystal Palace. I expect there will be a lot more as we get into the transfer window but I suppose if Kandol goes back to Leeds, we will need a replacement.

It was good to read that John Berylson wants to stay at the club for the next twenty-five years and maybe hand over to his son. It is what a club like ours needs, something stable at the top. That is what we had with Reg Burr and we had a pretty successful club then, so I hope he does.

What a cheek getting vouchers that we have to exchange for tickets at a pre-arranged destination when we go to Leeds. It is about time we made things difficult for them like they always do for us.

Now the game is on Monday night maybe it will be better staying home and watching it on Sky and upset Leeds by not going again but that won't help the team.

* * *

26 December 2008, Peterborough United 1 – 0 Millwall

Not the sort of Boxing Day result we wanted, losing 1-0 at Peterborough and having Tony Craig sent off. We need to do better on Sunday against Yeovil.

* * *

28 December 2008, Millwall 1 – 1 Yeovil Town

Well we did but only just. We should have gone on and scored loads after Robinson opened the scoring. The first twenty minutes were great and we should have had a hatful of goals. Then we turned off again and we were lucky to get away with a 1-1 draw.

We seem to be going backwards but at least we are still third in the table. Hope we start the New Year in a more positive way.

JANUARY

Start of the transfer window and we get a huge wage off the books with Ryan Smith going to Southampton. I know we did not get any money for him but his contract was up in the summer and we need to save cash now. I can't understand what happened to him. Was it Donachie moving him to the right wing or is he just the sort of player who flatters to deceive?

* * *

3 January 2009, Millwall 2 – 2 Crewe Alexandra

I said the cup game against Crewe would be different but it was just the score that was. A 2-2 draw was not a reflection on the game and although both Laird and Frampton scored scrappy goals, Crewe's goals were just as bad from a defensive point of view and as usual two poor refereeing decisions helped them to score.

Can't say how we will do in the replay as we always seem to struggle against Crewe but a match at either Hull or Newcastle must give the players that bit extra.

The big question of the day though is where was Zak Whitbread? He might have been injured but there was no mention of that anywhere so are we about to sell him, leaving him out of the side means he is not cup-tied? He is also on four bookings and with Craig still banned and Robinson missing the next game as well, it might be that he was kept out so that he did not get booked, that would mean we would have all our central defenders missing for the next game except for Frampton.

It was good to see Scott Barron play in the last two matches as well. He did not look out of place and I thought he did well. However, we have now lost Bolder and Moore who both go back to their respective clubs. I hope we get them back again or we need to buy players as good or better.

* * *

We are looking at a striker from Stevenage and a midfield player at Shrewsbury. Not sure if we need another midfield player but if Bolder is not coming back then we will. We will also need a striker if Kandol goes back and there are always players to pick up in the lower leagues, so who knows?

Well done Cheltenham for getting Saturday's match called off early. It is about time somebody got their act together and stopped us from travelling. The problem for us now is that Robinson and Craig will miss the cup match at Crewe on Tuesday instead of the league game and that will make it harder for us.

* * *

Shame that Crewe's game was called off as well as it might have helped if they were tired from a game at the weekend.

Now we are looking at a couple of players in Ireland. It has been quiet so far on the transfer scene so I hope we are not going to leave things until the end of the transfer window and then take on some dross just to get somebody in.

Goodbye Dave Brammer. I liked you and you did well for us. Hope all goes well for you at Port Vale. Still that is another one of the top earners gone and only Pidgely left to go.

* * *

13 January 2009, English FA Cup, Crewe Alexandra 2 – 3 Millwall

History was made tonight with Harris finally breaking Sheringham's goal scoring record. Well done Neil on making it 112 and I hope there is a lot more. Add Barron's first goal ever and Whitbread's winner and a nice 2-3 win over Crewe to take us to Hull and also put us in the mood for Tranmere on Saturday.

Well we got a striker but not the one I was expecting. Izale McLeod could be a good loan and we have him until the end of the season. I thought we missed out on him when he went to Charlton but we could never have afforded him then. So does that mean that Kandol is on his way back to Leeds?

* * *

Now we have taken another midfield player and striker on trial. We are certainly looking but will we end up taking on anyone and if so how good will they be? I must admit I have been impressed with Jacket's signings so far although he has had a few useless ones along the way.

* * *

17 January 2009, Millwall 1 – 0 Tranmere Rovers

Nice to see the club present Harris with recognition of his goal scoring as soon as we could and not wait until the end of the season. It set us up nicely for the win against Tranmere although it was a hard game and to be honest Laird's goal was the best bit of football all afternoon.

Still, it is another three points. McLeod looked lively when he came on and will be a good asset. Shame he hit the post and did not score but I think he will get a few for us before the season ends.

Shame about Barron though, he wasn't even on the bench and I thought he did really well for us when he played. Nice one Tresor. Saying you want to stay permanently will help but a lot of fans see you as a lazy player. I know that is your style and you help to vary our play. I would like to keep you but I do not think you'll come for free and I am not sure we can afford to buy you.

Good news about Ashley Grimes signing a new two-and-a-half-year contract. I like the way he plays a lot and I think next season he will come into his own. Kenny Jackett is using him just right as far as I'm concerned.

At least it was an injury that kept Barron out of the side last Saturday and not that he was dropped. With Whitbread suspended for the Hull game as well it might be difficult but I still think we can do well there.

* * *

24 January 2009, English FA Cup, Hull City 2 – 0 Millwall

Okay we lost, but 2-0 is not the end of the world when you consider we were playing away against a Premier League side and Mr Attwell was not the best of referees to have on the day, but when has that been any different?

The worrying thing is the trouble in the crowd and the Hull chairman blaming us. Well we might have been in the fight but with the kiosks in the ground closed for us and with everyone being searched on the way in, the missiles thrown at the beginning could have only come from one place.

My other concern is how did so-called 'known' troublemakers get tickets and why was pay on the day allowed? I think Hull need to own up to that problem, as well as where the fans were placed and the policing/stewarding on the day. Still, we are an easy target as usual.

The news is out. There were twelve arrests, eleven of them Hull supporters. Says it all I think. However, we must not get complacent as we do have a hooligan element in the club, like every other club does.

* * *

27 January 2009, Hereford 0 – 2 Millwall

It seems that Leeds does not want Kandol but the big question is, do we? If we do, can we afford him? The papers say we are still after Scowcroft and also Carl Fletcher from Palace, but I think I'll just wait and see what happens.

A good 0-2 win at Hereford but with the goals coming from Craig and Laird, I am getting a bit worried about our strikers not scoring. I know goals from all over the team are a good thing but we need goals from the strikers or things will start going wrong.

* * *

That is Kandol back at Leeds and I don't think we'll be seeing him back at The Den. I bet he plays his first game for Leeds against us and scores the winner.

Preston Edwards has gone to Dover on a month's loan and that should do him good. I think he'll have a part to play next season and he can do with some first team experience no matter where it is.

I am glad Adam Bolder is back and this time on a permanent deal. I know a lot of fans are not sure about him but I think he will give us a bit of stability in the middle. I am a bit surprised about this half time smoking area that the club are giving a trial to. At least they are listening to the fans but after the two-match trial will it be stopped on some spurious excuse. We can only wait and see.

At least Kandol won't score against us when we play Leeds, as he has gone on loan to Charlton. Darren Ward has gone there too, shame for both of them.

* * *

31 January 2009, Millwall 1 – 2 Scunthorpe United
We had enough chances to beat Scunthorpe and although Alexander scored our goal he could have had at least three more. Their two were well taken but we made two poor defensive errors to give them the goals.

FEBRUARY

With Grabban having a hamstring injury and Robinson breaking his foot, it is all happening at the wrong time for us. Still we have until five o'clock tomorrow to bring others in so we will have to wait and see what happens.

I was sorry to hear that Marc Bircham has had to stop playing through injury. He did a good job for us while he was here.

Adrian Forbes goes to Grimsby on loan until the end of the season and we bring in a defender, Richard Duffy, on loan from Portsmouth. We needed a defender with Robinson out for a long time and Duffy can play at right back or centre back so not too bad a choice. I suppose that means we can't expect Senda or Robinson back before the end of the season now. I must say I was surprised we did not bring in another striker but we can still make loan signings for a while so maybe that is the thinking behind that.

I am not sure if the Colchester game being called off because of snow is a good or bad thing. Bad because we needed to get straight back on the winning trail but good because it gives us time to sort things out before the Leeds game.

The rumours are that we are still after Scowcroft. Maybe we will make a move for him when the loan window opens again on Monday. We really can do with a striker that can put the ball into the back of the net.

* * *

9 February 2009, Leeds United 2 – 0 Millwall
What a good idea to make Tony Craig captain while Robinson is out. He has got a lot of passion and won't stand for any nonsense so that should keep the ball rolling nicely.

We were robbed 2-0 by Leeds. We had nearly all the possession and they still scored twice. Beckford's first goal was a beauty but he should have been sent off for the elbow in Forde's face long before his second. We should have had a penalty and I am not sure if Alexander's header was over the line or not but I'll give the officials the benefit of the doubt on that one.

Duffy had a steady debut until he got a dead leg and could be a good acquisition, but we must start getting our strikers scoring regularly or we will find ourselves slipping out of the play-off zone.

A Gong for Bomber? I'll go along with that. Well done South London Press for even suggesting the idea. Services to Millwall, football and charity, that should be enough to get him something, but I bet it won't happen.

* * *

So Beckford has been charged by the FA for the foul on Forde. Glad to see that they take these things seriously and a three-match ban for him will certainly be a blow for the team, and to think he said nothing happened when everybody could see it. Leeds have got a cheek saying that it only happened because the game was televised, so what are they saying that he should have got away with it? Mind you he would have had the game not been on TV.

We have signed another midfield player on loan, James Henry from Reading for a month. I don't know why we need another right-winger but it indicates that both Grabban and Hackett won't be fit enough to play for a while.

There are rumours that Dunne is off to Charlton. He won't be missed by a lot of fans if he goes but we have a problem with defenders at the moment so keeping him until the end of the season seems prudent to me.

* * *

14 February 2009, Stockport County 2 – 2 Millwall
Two up at Stockport and we end up drawing 2-2. McLeod's goals came at the right time and he should have had at least one more penalty but as usual the referee looked the other way when it happened. In addition, Johnson stamped on Craig, so he should not have been on the pitch to score the equaliser.

The referee did not worry about sending Martin off for his second yellow card though and that was a big part of the problem for letting the lead slip. Henry made a promising debut though.

* * *

17 February 2009, Millwall 1 – 1 Swindon Town
What a goal. Henry's equaliser was amazing and we won't see a better goal this season. Swindon's goal was due to poor defending. However, we have to get our strikers scoring and the team as a whole needs to work out how to break down sides that defend high up the pitch.

We are supposed to be looking at a loan of a Premier League striker. Well we certainly need somebody who can put the ball in the net so let's hope the rumour is true and we get a good one.

* * *

Vincent Pericard!! Is that a joke? He is only in the Premiership because he is at Stoke. He never seemed much when he has played against us in the past but I hope I'm wrong.

* * *

21 February 2009, Millwall 0 – 1 Brighton and Hove Albion

Wouldn't you know it? Brighton get rid of Micky Adams in the morning and then they win with the only shot they get on target. We had so many chances it was untrue and we still could not put one away.

Pericard made his debut but I did say he was not the answer. I might be a bit harsh there and should give him a couple of games to prove his worth but then neither is McLeod or Harris, although at least he puts in a workmanlike shift.

* * *

24 February 2009, Cheltenham Town 1 – 3 Millwall

A good win at Cheltenham but we made hard work of it in the first half, and it was only with the half time changes that things began to work for us. Henry took the penalty well, Grimes scored one and made Laird's so maybe he should start on Saturday.

I said Pericard was not the answer for us and he won't be now, although I did not mean it to happen that way. He tore his calf muscle last night and that is him finished for the season. He goes back to Stoke and with Hackett and Dunne injured in training on Monday and Bolder being sick during the match, things are going against us again.

Still we have moved up to fourth in the table and we can still make the automatic promotion positions, but we need to keep getting results now.

I think staying at Dover for another month will be good experience for Preston Edwards and maybe he should add another one as well. He will certainly come into the reckoning next season when Pidgely goes, as I am sure he will. Shame about Danny Senda needing another operation and that means he has not played all season. Hope he comes back all right, like Chris Hackett did this season.

By the way, what is happening about all the players that are out of contract at the end of this season? Shouldn't we be doing something about them?

* * *

28 February 2009, Millwall 2 – 3 Oldham Athletic

We must sort out our defence. They seem to be okay and then play like they did today against Oldham. We give away two soft goals in the first nine minutes, Harris and Grimes' wonder goal get us level, and then we give away another soft one in the 93rd minute. You would have thought we would have learnt by now.

Still the soccer gods must be looking on us favourably at the moment as all our main rivals lost as well.

MARCH

Just what is Izale McLeod playing at? I thought he had a big ego and storming out of the ground before the Oldham game because he was not on the bench proves it. I did not think much of what I saw anyway but who knows what will happen with him now. Watch this space.

* * *

3 March 2009, Southend United 0 – 1 Millwall
Welcome back Gary Alexander. Your goal at Southend has put us back on track. It was good to see Adam Bolder back and Jimmy Abdou looked as if he could play at right back, although I think I would prefer an established full back there.

McLeod is done up like a kipper. He can't go back to Charlton and does not want to play for us. We should not pay his wages but I bet we end up having to; his trouble is, his ego is bigger than his talent.

* * *

7 March 2009, Huddersfield Town 1 – 2 Millwall
Another good away win at Huddersfield and good goals from Henry and Laird, about time we scored late in the game. The trouble is we are still not getting goals from our strikers although to be fair Jackett is not picking them to start games. Only Alexander started today.

* * *

10 March 2009, Millwall 1 – 0 Northampton Town
What went wrong? We got a decent referee and the fact that he allowed play to go on for the foul on Henry brought about Alexander's goal. Shame the referee did not go back and book the Northampton player though.

We totally outplayed them and should have scored more but we are still missing too many chances. We need a twenty-goal-a-season man for next season, but where do you find one?

I am glad James Henry's loan has been extended. We have come on a bundle since he arrived. Shame he won't be available for the playoff final though so we will have to get automatic promotion instead.

McLeod is back as he could not play for anyone else, dead money for him now that we have still got to pay him. Surely we can't play him in the side though as I am sure the fans won't like it and more importantly how will the other players react? I have just seen that Tony Warner will play in goal for Leicester tomorrow and with Dyer and Hayles in their side as well, the old boy brigade will be out in force.

* * *

14 March 2009, Millwall 0 – 1 Leicester City
A goal each and hitting the woodwork each is a fair result against Leicester. Shame it wasn't like that. We didn't get the goal and they got a soft one. Same old story too many missed chances. Where is the goal scorer that can put them away?

Why did the idiots have to show up today? Throwing stuff on the pitch won't help us at all. Why don't they just go away and find another club to bring shame on? We do not want them here.

We need to do something at MK Dons tomorrow night but I hope Jackett resists the temptation to bring McLeod back into the side. He really is not the answer and I am sure he will disrupt the others if he plays.

* * *

17 March 2009, Milton Keynes Dons 0 – 1 Millwall
Still no striker scoring but what a win. Laird has started to put the ball in the net regularly now so that is good. At least we are getting goals from all over the team.

I do not understand why the club want to move the family enclosure yet again. Still, prices for next season have been frozen which is good news and so is lowering the senior fan age from sixty-five to sixty.

* * *

21 March 2009, Hartlepool United 2 – 3 Millwall
It was heart in the mouth time at Hartlepool but what a game. Forde saves a penalty, then we go two down, Harris comes on at half time and scores a hat-trick in ten minutes. Who said he was past it?

It was good to see Grabban back but a shame about Henry. We seem to get one fit just to lose another. Still Dunne, Hackett and Spiller are back in training so things are looking up.

Could Jason Price be the answer to our goal scoring needs? We have seen strikers come and go on loan here all season and none have been any good except Kandol, so here's hoping he not only scores the goals we are missing but also manages to stay until his loan runs out at the end of the season.

* * *

28 March 2009, Crewe Alexandra 0 – 1 Millwall

Well he got off to a good start when he replaced broken nose victim Neil Harris at Crewe, scoring a very late winner. Keep this up Jason and you will be a hero with The Den faithful.

There is a meeting tonight with the season ticket holders that sit in the West Stand where the club want to move the family enclosure to. That should be interesting.

At last, new contracts have been offered to Alexander, Barron, Frampton and, as a surprise for many, Harris. Hope they all sign up for next season. There are still another nine out of contract when this season ends so what is going to happen to them?

It is good to see Berylson is still happy at the club even though we are still losing money. Stability is something that we have needed for a long time, in fact since Reg Burr went, and maybe we have found it at last. I certainly hope the hooligan factor does not come back to haunt us and spoil things again.

* * *

31 March 2009, Millwall 0 – 1 Colchester United

Another late goal when losing to Colchester, another dodgy referee and Alexander has fourteen stitches in his face. We still had enough chances to win the game though, we only have ourselves to blame in the end.

APRIL

I thought moving the family enclosure would cause problems. It seems those sitting in the West Stand do not want to move, and why should they, and those in the East Stand do not want to either. What will happen next? The club would do well just to abandon the idea.

Ticketmaster goes at the end of this season and I must say it has taken too long to do it. Bringing in our own system, Seethreesixty (what a strange name), might sort out a lot of the ticketing problems but I will hold judgement on that until after it has been in service for a while.

Neil Harris has signed his new one-year contract but the others are still in talks about theirs. Talk about a striker from Stevenage, Steve Morison, signing next season. We will just have to wait and see.

* * *

4 April 2009, Millwall 3 – 1 Walsall

Two goals from Alexander, even with his stitched face and another from Price gave us a good 3-1 win over Walsall even if the game was not that great, but three points is three points and we can still grab that second spot.

Stay where you are. Move if you want to. Pay whatever price you like as well by the sounds of it. Season ticket holders should be treated better than this. What is this club up to?

* * *

10 April 2009, Yeovil Town 2 – 0 Millwall

Dunne sent off and losing 2-0 at Yeovil has put a big dent in our automatic promotion push. We really do need a win against Peterborough on Monday night now.

* * *

13 April 2009, Millwall 2 – 0 Peterborough United

What a game. What a win. What a referee, and that goes for his assistant as well. A penalty missed twice by Alexander, both taken again, needs a lot of courage by the officials and maybe the fact that the game was live on Sky might have had something to do with it but who cares. Martin scored at the third time of asking. The Peterborough goalkeeper should have stayed on his line. Price's goal was the icing on the cake and we were completely dominant. If we play like this for the rest of the season then we could still go up in second place.

Gary Alexander deserves his Community Player of the Year award as he does a lot for the club in his spare time.

Another tour of Ireland and a testimonial match for Richard Sadlier for pre-season. It's about time Sadlier got his testimonial. Hope the opposition are good.

Well done Andy Frampton for winning the player of the year award. He has a lot of detractors but I think he is an honest player who gives his all and deserves the award.

* * *

18 April 2009, Bristol Rovers 4 – 2 Millwall

It is the playoffs only now after losing 4-2 at Bristol Rovers. Alexander was harshly sent off and we should appeal against that one. Without the resulting penalty it could have been difference, especially as Harris hit the bar between Abdou's two goals. We might just have managed to at least grab a point.

Alexander's red card has been rescinded, which is good for him and us, but it does not give us the goals back or the chance of gaining at least a point.

CYC and Oppida are staying as sponsors next season. That is good to hear and shows that the club are doing something right at last. That must make Mr Berylson very happy.

After all these years the club does something right and puts tickets for the play-off semi finals on sale with more than just a few days to scramble to buy one. They are also going to get next year's kit out in May and that makes a change to getting it in September. I am impressed.

* * *

25 April 2009, Millwall 2 – 1 Leyton Orient
Another penalty save from Forde and two good goals from Alexander. Orient might have gone in front but they were no match for us. Just how did Henry get that cross over for Alexander's second goal? What a shame he won't be playing in the play-off final if we get there.

Good to hear that Frampton and Barron have now signed new contracts. That should help settle their minds before the play-offs arrive. Just hope Alexander does the same.

* * *

He has signed. So now what about the others? I have got my own theory about who will go and who will stay but I don't think telling anyone before the play-offs will be a good thing, especially if they are going.

MAY

2 May 2009, Carlisle United 2 – 0 Millwall
So we finished fifth. I did not think we would lose at Carlisle so 2-0 was a bit of a shock. So it is Leeds and another voucher day but I don't mind the first leg at home. It might work out best for us. Roll on next Saturday.

It was no surprise to hear that Danny Spiller was being let go. He could probably have done a job for us but he has never really recovered from the injury he got when he came here so it is probably best that he finds somewhere else. Telling him won't affect the rest of the squad so all the best Danny.

* * *

Oh no! Price gets injured and that will probably be him out for the other two games as well.

Left: Gary Alexander takes aim in the play-off final against Scunthorpe. (*Brian Tonks*)

Below: Gary Alexander jumps for joy after his spectacular equaliser. (*Brian Tonks*)

* * *

9 May 2009, League One Play-Offs Semi-Final 1, Millwall 1 – 0 Leeds United
However, all clouds have a silver lining and Harris came in and got the goal that puts us in front when we go to their place next Thursday. Will 1-0 be enough? Most people will say no but I think it will. Just believe.

* * *

14 May 2009, League One Play-Offs Semi-Final 2, Leeds United 1 – 1 Millwall (1-2 on aggregate)
Jimmy Abdou, Jimmy Abdou. What a game. What a save. What a goal. What a result.

Do I sound like I'm repeating myself? Too bad, I can't get over the result. 1-1 was just magic and a great save by Forde to stop Beckford's penalty. What a way to get your own back for the elbow in the face in the league match.

No mention about the coins thrown on the pitch then, or the damage Leeds fans made to all the cars after the game. Why did I expect any?

So we have got our striker for next season. Don't know much about Steve Morison but he scored a lot of goals for Stevenage. It is a big step up but we have taken on non-league players before with good results.

* * *

I'VE GOT MY WEMBLEY TICKET.

I am glad Kenny Jackett has told the team that they will be the basis of next season's squad. That should settle their minds before the final on Sunday.

* * *

24 May 2009, League One Play-Off Final, Millwall 2 – 3 Scunthorpe United
I can't believe it. One down, we hit the post and then Alexander puts us one in front. His first must be the goal of the season. I am still rubbing my eyes over that forty-yard strike.

Actually it might be because of his six yard miss in the second half and the fact that we then lost the game to another goal in the last five minutes, and we have another season in League One. We have never been able to sort out that problem.

It will be hard but bring it on.

CHAPTER FIVE

TWISTS, TURNS AND PROMOTION, SEASON 2009/2010

CLOSED SEASON

Wow! Ten players released. I thought most of those on the list would go but I must admit I was surprised about Danny Senda and Marcus Bignot. How can you put Senda on the list and not Bignot? Still I am sure Jackett knows what he is doing, well I hope so.

I hope Edwards re-signs though as I think he will have a good future with the club even if he's not quite ready yet. He will certainly make a good number two to Forde.

* * *

That is an interesting rule change for next season having to have four home grown players in the squad for each game. Still, with seven substitutes I think that might be abused a bit and a home grown player that is never going to get off the bench will be on it, at least at some clubs.

I am a bit surprised about Heather Rabbatts standing down as CEO. I thought she would see it through to the end of the regeneration at least. Still, she is staying on as a non-executive director and I guess she has plenty of work to do. With Andy Ambler taking the role temporarily I wonder who will take it on in the end. I wouldn't rule Ambler out for the job.

I am glad Jackett has told Senda he can earn a contract if he proves his fitness, so now it is up to you Danny.

The rumour mill is at it already – £1 million for Martin and £1.5 million for Whitbread? The money is good I suppose but do we really want to sell either of them? I don't think so. Also it is good to hear that Alan Dunne has signed a new one-year contract and better still that Kenny Jackett has signed a new three-year one. However, the signing of a new goalkeeper in John Sullivan from Brighton leaves me wondering what Preston Edwards will do now.

* * *

More good news, well I hope it is. Peter De Savoury's shares have been bought by another American, Bill Shenkman, which means Lacey can't get them. My only thought now is will Shenkman be a Berylson or a Lacey. Only time will tell I suppose.

The good news keeps coming. The FA is taking no action over the 'crowd invasion' in the Leeds play-off match and I should think so too. I am glad that two arrests were made and hope they both don't see the inside of The Den again, well at least for a while, but the rest of the mob, all twenty odd of them, were just celebrating Harris' goal.

I think I know what Edwards will do now that he has been offered a new contract with a pay cut. It won't encourage him to stay that is for sure and he can go for a free as well, which is a shame. I hope we do not come up against him during the season.

However, I am getting bored with all the rumours about who is going or arriving so let's just wait and see. The current one is Ben Davies of Shrewsbury. I'm not sure if we need another midfield player but if he does come then he needs to be an asset.

* * *

Silly season starts now with the players coming back for pre-season but I'm glad we have finally managed to sort out Richard Sadlier's testimonial. Middlesbrough will be good opponents just before the season starts and you never know Colin Cooper might even play for a bit.

Berylson was not joking when he said we would be striker rich, now that Jason Price has signed a one-year contract. I wonder who will end up being the top scorer and how Kenny Jackett will use them all. I hope Adrian Forbes does well at Grimsby as he did all right for us when we needed him.

Is this some kind of a joke? Paul Ifill is training with us. That is not too bad but are we thinking of signing him? Watch this space but I hope not. There are plenty of players I would put in the list before him but football is a funny old game as we all know.

Just getting to the sharp end and all of a sudden we have three central defenders out. I was looking forward to seeing if Pat O'Conner would break into the first team and now he is out all season with a knee injury. Then Robbo needs another operation on his foot and Whitbread injures his thigh. Still it would not be Millwall if things like this didn't happen.

* * *

Now Whitbread turns down a new contract and we put him on the transfer list. Whoever gets him will get one hell of a defender but I hope we get plenty of money for him as Liverpool get half of any money we make.

We really do need to look at getting a defender in now as it is all going wrong before it starts.

First pre-season friendly over and a 0-1 win at Dagenham and Redbridge. Okay, they are not the best in the world but this is all about getting ready for the season and the fact that Alexander scored might just clear his mind about the miss at Wembley. Mind you he missed a penalty – again. Please don't let him take them during the season.

No Ifill then as he wants too much money, he is off to Wellington Phoenix. I hope he likes the New Zealand sunshine as the football won't be up to much – say no more. I am also glad that Joe Gallen has signed a new three-year deal. It shows that both he and Kenny Jackett are committed to the club and we need some stability after all the turmoil we have had over the last few seasons.

* * *

Off to Ireland for a short tour and a good 0-4 win at Galway. Alexander, Harris, Hackett and Grimes got the goals, and as I hoped goals would come from all over the squad this season, this will be a good indication that they might. Let's see how they do at Shelbourne on Tuesday.

* * *

Okay, it was a 0-1 win at Shelbourne and an own goal at that. Still a win is a win and also a confidence booster so I will take that.

Just seen Richard Duffy has signed for Exeter. He did not really do much for us but maybe he will find life better there. We will see when we play against them.

Another good 2-1 win against Stevenage and Morison is now off the mark with both goals against his old club. I hope he does well this season but he seems to be trying too hard to impress.

A one-month contract has been accepted by Danny Senda and an incentive to get a better one by showing what he can do. Well done Danny, prove your fitness, you deserve a longer contract.

The idea of naming a stand after Neil Harris is a good one but then why not a Sheringham stand as well, and I still think there should be one named after Reg Burr.

* * *

Another good 4-1 win against Dartford and the goals were shared around again. Harris, two for Price, and Senda getting the best of them all, were the scorers. Senda played 90 minutes as well so let's hope that he is near the end of his long road to recovery.

The other good thing is that we have only let in two goals and both of those were penalties so that must bring confidence as well. We have got our first

Team for the 2009/2010 season. *(Chris Bethell)*

defender in, Jack Smith, who has been playing here on trial after being let go by Swindon. He signed until January so has time to get an extended one.

AUGUST

At last, Richard Sadlier gets his testimonial game and a 1-1 draw against Middlesbrough. Yes I know ours was an own goal but Alexander's header might have gone in.

We really do have a defender crisis now with Craig injuring himself in the match and Senda doing the same when he came on to replace him. I hope neither of them are too serious but it is a good job we signed Smith.

* * *

What bad luck for Senda, just back and now out again until the end of the year with an Achilles heel problem that will need surgery. He was only on the pitch for ten minutes having replaced Craig. At least he won't be out for too long.

Danny Spiller found himself a place at Wycombe Wanderers. Should be interesting to see how the crowd react when we play them here.

The season starts tomorrow and we could be in all sorts of problems defensively. Robinson, Craig and Senda are definitely out, Whitbread is probably out and now Frampton might not make it either. Oh well here goes.

* * *

8 August 2009, Southampton 1 – 1 Millwall

A 1-1 draw at Southampton and the television audience will see that we mean business this season as well. I thought their goal was offside but a great one from Abdou and how could the linesmen say the ball was out before Alexander scored?

By the way I know I did not want Alexander to take penalties this season but why did Dunne take it, resulting in an inevitable miss? I thought Smith and Morison had decent debuts but has Price injured his hamstring? Things never go right for us do they?

* * *

11 August 2009, English League Cup, Millwall 4 – 0 Bournemouth

What a win in the first round of the Carling Cup and our first home game of the season. A 4-0 win and Bournemouth did not know what hit them when we unveiled our new 4-3-3 formation. A good goal from Alexander and a great hat-trick from Harris, although the team played some terrific football. Hope we keep this up.

We have brought in a second defender in George Friend on a month's loan from Wolves and he can also play in midfield. He is left footed as well and we need one of those.

We've drawn 'the Hampsters' (West Ham) away in the next round of the Carling Cup and already all the talk is about the fights that will happen and not the football. It is ridiculous and so are the number of tickets we have been given, just 1,500. That is the way to start fights.

The 'flying pig' arrives with his new Carlisle teammates at The Den tomorrow and I hope he lets in a few.

* * *

15 August 2009, Millwall 0 – 0 Carlisle United

Now I wish I hadn't made that last comment as the game ended 0-0, although we hit the woodwork three times. Never mind it is still early in the season. George Friend made a steady debut.

We have drawn Barnet away in the Johnstone's Paint Trophy. That could be an interesting team selection.

We won't be saying goodbye to Zak Whitbread then, well at least not until January, he had an operation on his thigh and won't be back until November. You never know, we might get a few games out of him yet.

* * *

18 August 2009, Millwall 2 – 0 Oldham Athletic
A good win over Oldham, but I'm not sure if 2-0 was the right result. Martin and Harris took their goals well, plus another penalty saved from Forde. He is certainly becoming a master at that.

Is Kenny Jackett experimenting with the formation or is he going to change it according to the team we play against and then alter it again during the match? Interesting! Thought I would also mention it was a typical Andy D'Urso game. Enough said!

We have been given another 800 tickets for the West Ham match. Nowhere near enough in my view and that could still spell trouble from the idiots that will turn up without tickets.

I don't think I am too great a fan of buying tickets for the game online. I know that was only for the initial allocation and not the additional 800 but I have a dodgy feeling about it.

* * *

21 August 2009, Southend United 0 – 0 Millwall
No goals and a draw at Southend, although we did hit the woodwork again. We changed to a 4-3-3 formation to start the game and it looks like Jackett is going to change the formation depending on the opponents, where we are playing, etc. I do not mind that especially as he is not afraid to alter it during the match if it is not working. He did this tonight when he changed to 4-4-2 when Hackett and Harris came on.

I would also like to know why the new away strip is not available for the players. I like the white shirts we played in tonight but if we have a second strip then surely the manufacturers should be held to account if they can't get it to us.

Oh well, onto Tuesday's game now. I hope we put on a good performance even if we do lose.

* * *

25 August 2009, English League Cup, West Ham United 3 – 1 Millwall (aet)
What a great performance it was and to think that if we had been able to hang on for just three more minutes Harris' goal would have been the winner.

The penalty was a dodgy decision, though I suppose we should be used to them by now, and they were always going to get the third after the second went in. Well played the Lions, you were a credit to the club and did not look out of place at all. As a club we must be in trouble with injuries though as we could only name four substitutes. I know Friend was not allowed to play because Wolves don't want him cup-tied, but if we have that many injuries at this time of the season we need to bring in more loan players or hope the injured ones get better very quickly.

Unfortunately, the same can't be said for what went on outside the ground. I will reserve judgement until I hear more about that, although it was not us that went onto the pitch and if West Ham gets away with it happening three times then there is no justice.

Everything I have heard, seen and read say it was not us that started the trouble and that makes a change. I'm not daft enough to think that there were no Millwall fans involved in the fighting somewhere along the line but it certainly seems that West Ham were the main culprits in all that went on outside the ground and I hope whoever it is, and I include Millwall fans, get severely punished when this is put to bed.

* * *

The ramifications about Tuesday are still going on and I expect it will for a long time. I hope the FA and the two clubs sort out what went wrong and why. Of course the police have a part to play in that as well and that includes the racist chants that Cole and Price were supposed to have received.

Just what is wrong with these people? Don't they realise that time has moved on and that decent fans do not want the name of their club dragged into things like this.

So what will happen next? Nothing to do but wait and see I suppose. I just hope there is no hangover for the game tomorrow against Brighton.

* * *

28 August 2009, Millwall 1 – 1 Brighton and Hove Albion
Looks like there was, we took an early lead through Price and should have been at least three up at half time. Things went wrong from then on in and we were lucky to get away with a 1-1 draw in the end. Was Tuesday a factor? I think it might have been. Mind you we had our usual bad refereeing decisions. Whing should have gone for his second bad tackle on Martin, Price should have had a penalty and how no official saw their goalkeeper handle outside the area will be a mystery forever.

Young Kiernan Hughes-Mason had a good ten minutes when he made his debut and looks like a good prospect, but what happened to Harris? He was named in the starting line-up but did not feature at all.

* * *

That is the answer about Harris, strained a calf muscle in the warm up and with Hackett straining his groin on Tuesday we will be lucky to be able to put a side out soon.

It was nice to hear that the club are sorting things with the fan, and his family, that was stabbed at West Ham and that they are all keeping it quiet. I can't wait to find out what the FA will do about the two clubs.

SEPTEMBER

Transfer deadline day and although we are desperate for defenders all we get is a midfield player, Danny Schofield, on a two-year deal from Yeovil. I think we were after him before.

Anyway Robbo's back tonight so maybe things are turning round. At least we only need to name five substitutes in this competition so that helps.

* * *

1 September 2009, Johnstone's Paint Trophy, Barnet 2 – 0 Millwall

Me and my big mouth, lost to Barnet 2-0 but that is all right as I am not that fussed about the Johnstone's Paint Trophy. Keeping the unbeaten streak going in the league must be our priority. However, losing Robinson again really is a problem and it looks like he will be out for some time again, and with Price injured in the game as well things are not looking good at the moment. It was not the best match for Sullivan to make his debut in.

Having a lot of injuries near the end of the season is bad enough but having them at the beginning is really going to hurt us. Ten players out for the game at Bristol Rovers and now we have added no strikers to our lack of defenders. Maybe we just pack the side with midfield players and hope.

Mind you this could be the chance Ashley Grimes is looking for or maybe one of the youngsters will shine through, or somebody plays with a lot of painkillers. We will just have to wait and see.

* * *

5 September 2009, Bristol Rovers 2 – 0 Millwall

Well it did not work as we lost 2-0. Schofield and Marquis made their debuts and the young striker tried hard but he has still got a lot to learn. In addition, now we have added Laird and Alexander to the injury list.

At least the red and black away strip is here at last, didn't do us any good though.

The transfer window for loans opens tomorrow and I hope the rumours about Henry and Ward are true, and with players starting to come back from injury things might start to go in the right direction. Watch out you 'Gills!'

One down and one to go; we have signed James Henry until December.

* * *

12 September 2009, Gillingham 2 – 0 Millwall

Two down. Darren Ward has signed until the end of the year. It will be interesting to see what happens then with both of them.

Okay, the Gills won. I suppose 2-0 was not a bad score in the end but we did not play well at all and I should have known that Curtis Weston would score against us. That does not mean we should have booed the side like some of the fans did. It is encouragement they need at the moment.

Ward and Henry both played, although the injury hoodoo is still here as Henry and the returning Harris have joined the list now. At least Morison and Hackett have made it back.

Goodbye George Friend, back to Wolves after your loan with us. You did a job but you were nothing exceptional and I do not think we will be asking you back.

* * *

19 September 2009, Millwall 3 – 1 Huddersfield Town

Will this injury problem never go away? Now Grimes has pulled a hamstring. Just what is going on with our players? Is it the training or the physiotherapy or just plain bad luck?

I did not expect that. What a great win against Huddersfield. Three goals and yes we let them have one back, as usual, but Ward was knackered by that time. What a goal by Hackett and a great idea to let him roam anywhere. Harris took his goal well too and at last Morison is off the mark. He does not seem match fit but that can be said for at least half of the side at the moment.

The Tacheback campaign was well supported and so was testicle day. Why don't we ever get the good press we deserve about things like this?

I cannot believe the FA has charged us with three things after the Hamsters game. Maybe I'll concede the racial chants to Cole, although he did incite the fans. I'm glad to hear that the club are going to contest the charges and so they should. How can a club be responsible for their fans when they are not in their ground? It seems to me that charging us with the same things as them, apart from the pitch invasions, is a way of watering down what they did.

* * *

26 September 2009, Leyton Orient 1 – 0 Millwall

We played very poorly at Leyton Orient and maybe we deserved to lose 1-0. We really must start winning away from home or at least picking up one point here and there.

* * *

29 September 2009, Millwall 0 – 0 Yeovil

A 0-0 draw at home to Yeovil was not what we were all hoping for. They were not a good side but they did work hard to stop us scoring and that is our problem. We need to put this right quickly. We did have a few chances though but should not they have had their player sent off for elbowing Forde? Mind you he was lucky not to have walked for pushing him in the face when he retaliated so I suppose that evened things up.

OCTOBER

I have just read that the club are taking legal advice over the charges the FA has brought against them and that could prove very interesting. They are talking about no away tickets being sold *ever* and that is not just us but for *all clubs* if you can be charged with not controlling your fans in somebody else's ground, a very interesting argument.

Zoom Bakayogo has signed for Tranmere. I wonder if he will play tomorrow and if he does, will he bring the ex-player hoodoo with him?

* * *

3 October 2009, Millwall 5 – 0 Tranmere
He didn't! A 5-0 win does not come very often and although they were poor, that does not take away the fact that we scored five, in fact we should have had a lot more. Surely Barnes can't stay in charge there for much longer?

Henry's hat-trick was class and Frampton and Morison both headed good goals. Broome getting sent off did not affect the result as it came so late in the game. All right it provided Henry with his hat-trick goal but seeing Jason McAteer get sent to the stands was very pleasant. Never did like him.

I suppose Reading could take Henry back before his loan ends but I hope not. He will learn a lot with us and that must be good for them when he does go back.

More added to the injury list with Ward and Fuseini but it was good to see Craig back. We really need to stay injury free for a while and we also need to question what is happening at training sessions that makes players keep getting injured.

* * *

10 October 2009, Swindon Town 1 – 1 Millwall
The 1-1 draw at Swindon was not a bad point in the end and what a good time for Danny Schofield to get his first goal for the club. He seems to be settling down now.

It was a shame that Morison and Harris both hit the post though and we were always going to get a player sent off to equal things up after their player went. Pity it had to be Frampton with our defensive problems but now we must start winning away, not just taking one point.

Things were back to normal this week though, a great referee last week and this week back to the poor ones. Oh well that is part and parcel of being a

Millwall fan I suppose or is it just being a football fan in general these days? Things seem to happen to our players in the same way buses come along. Not only does Frampton get a red card on Saturday but also an ankle injury that will keep him out for about six weeks. Could the Scott Barron run in the side start here?

* * *

What's going on? First of all we hear about Swindon defender Amankwaah having a go about Harris' cancer and as soon as it became public knowledge, and not from Harris I'm glad to say, he starts saying he was racially abused to justify himself. What a joke, it could only happen to us.

Well done John Berylson for putting your money in the defence of the club against the FA charges. About time somebody at board level showed they really cared about this club. Now it is up to us, the fans, to back him and get ourselves down to The Den. It will be a big crowd for Leeds and maybe Colchester but what then? Come on Lions fans, back this club and its chairman, and turn up for as many matches as you can.

* * *

What is going on at training on a Friday? Now Scott Barron is injured. So much for me predicting he would get a run in the side.

* * *

17 October 2009, Stockport County 0 – 4 Millwall
Welcome back Robbo and what a good goal to open the scoring at Stockport. Shame Harris had a penalty saved as we do not see players score four that often but I must not be greedy and settle for his hat-trick. What a booster for Saturday. Bring on Leeds!

* * *

I am getting a bit worried about Saturday. Not the game itself but the fans. Now we have appealed against the charges from the FA over the West Ham game, they will be looking at everything we do and maybe this is the wrong game to be next on the fixture list. I just hope I am wrong and the idiots do not come but we could be in real trouble.

I have just read that Andy Ambler feels the same as I do and with tickets being sold to anyone, who knows what might happen. All I can say is that I hope we do not cause any trouble and do not even run on the pitch, even if we score.

* * *

24 October 2009, Millwall 2 – 1 Leeds United

What a win and both Harris and Alexander's goal were very well taken. I thought we might be in trouble when they equalised but we were never in any real danger of losing, except when Kandol hit the bar near the end I suppose.

Well done to our fans. No pitch encroachment and no trouble that I saw apart from a bottle being thrown onto the pitch. Leeds fans threw seats though, but I suppose that will be our fault. It was them that caused the trouble at London Bridge and also when the pub at Surrey Quays was smashed up this morning. Lots of police there, they even had to send back 100 Leeds fans that were there without tickets. Says it all!

Nice cup draw, either Crawley or AFC Wimbledon at home. We should get through to the next round with that one.

I have just heard about the fan with the Galatasary shirt and the Leeds fans with the Ferencváros flag. Hope they all get what should be coming to them, at least a ban I hope.

* * *

It is AFC Wimbledon but what a poor excuse by the police to switch it to Monday evening. We have played matches when there has been a firework display at Blackheath before.

I know injuries are part and parcel of football but we seem to be getting more than our fair share at the moment and it does not seem to stop. Alexander's heel has flared up again and he will be out for weeks. Schofield has a calf niggle and Martin is ill, and we have not even reached Friday yet.

Good of the police to say that they are pleased with the way the club and supporters acted at the Leeds match. What a shame the newspapers won't print that information.

* * *

31 October 2009, Millwall 2 – 1 Colchester United

Another win and two great goals to do it with. When we went behind to that deflected goal I thought that might be it, especially with the poor referee we had, again, and the cheating they were doing. Why wasn't Lisbie booked for that blatant dive?

Anyway a scorcher from Dunne and although Hackett was brilliant, Jackett was proved right when he changed him for Henry. What a free kick. He has scored some great goals for us and that was another of them. How nice it is to have a good bench at last.

NOVEMBER

A twenty-month contract for Jack Smith and that is nothing more than he deserves. He has been outstanding since he came here and currently he is my player of the season. Hope I have not put the mockers on him now.

Oh no! Kenny Jackett's been nominated for manager of the month. He will probably win it as well so that is the end of our unbeaten run. Please give it to somebody else. Paul Ince would be great.

The club have been awarded the 'Kick It Out' Intermediate Standard award and we are the first Football League club to get it. Having also won the three Kickz awards as well, we are doing well off the pitch, as well as on it. I know I have said it before but why do things like this never get into the national press?

* * *

Jimmy Abdou has just signed a new three-year contract and that is great. We need to start working on the other players who have contracts finishing at the end of the season.

It seems that the wrong man has been identified as the Galatasary shirt wearer and Leeds fans have been giving him problems. Hope the police find the right one but why have Leeds fans taken things into their own hands. Just goes to show what they are really like.

* * *

I told you Jackett would win the manager of the month award so we are either out of the cup come Monday or we lose at Brentford. Mind you we could break the curse. I seem to remember Mark McGhee doing it.

We are off to Staines if we win against the real Dons tomorrow. Let us not mess it up boys.

* * *

9 November 2009, English FA Cup, Millwall 4 – 1 AFC Wimbledon

What a great attendance for a Monday night match (9453) and well done those 3339 Dons fans who were there. At least you saw the new WBA heavyweight champion, David Haye, and your goalkeeper make some great saves but we were too good for you in the end.

Harris, Price (2) and Schofield made sure we went through, although when you made it 2-1 near the end I thought you might pull off a draw. Still it was not to be, despite your gallant efforts.

Good to see Ward and Grimes make the bench. Things are starting to go in our favour at last.

* * *

Here we go again. Watch the Staines match get changed. Everyone and his dog are now in discussions about when, where and what time the game will take place and a decision is being made on Friday the 13th. Who is kidding whom?

No chance of us getting Henry on a permanent basis now as he has signed a new contract with Reading. Mind you he really is good enough and learning all the time so I am glad he is here for now and maybe he will stay until the end of the season this time.

At least Kenny Jackett says he wants to stay here, mind you I hope that is not a smokescreen and he is really after a move somewhere else.

* * *

14 November 2009, Brentford 2 – 2 Millwall

I cannot believe the Brentford game. There were enough incidents to end the match 10-10 with the woodwork being hit all over the place by both teams; a Harris goal disallowed; goalmouth scrambles; and going behind twice, especially to the wind assisted goal from the corner. Robinson scored a great header and another special Henry free kick, this time from an incredible distance and position. I just do not know how he does it.

Mind you we did not play well for the first hour or so but overall I suppose 2-2 was a fair result and that is eight matches unbeaten now. Let's just keep it going.

Okay, we have registered a loss of £5.2 million last season but at least it is less than the year before. Not much I grant you but it is going in the right direction.

Here is another thing you won't see in the national press. Brentford have just written to the club to extol the good behaviour of the Millwall fans. Thanks Brentford, hopefully a few more clubs will do the same and we will finally get rid of the bad reputation that haunts us.

Good to see we have finally found ourselves a committed chairman, since Reg Burr I suppose. So thanks John Berylson for saying you will put more money into the club. Now let's see it happen.

* * *

It is Friday, it is injury day and right on cue James Henry has a hamstring injury and Neil Harris has an injury to his back. What is going on? Friday training should be banned.

* * *

21 November 2009, Millwall 0 – 2 Wycombe Wanderers
It was the 'Help the Heroes' match today and what a way to show our appreciation to those who went to war in Afghanistan. The fans were great. This is another thing that national newspapers will never say about Millwall because it does not fit their image of us as a nasty set of people. Look everyone, we really are a decent set of fans.

As far as the game was concerned we were awful and fully deserved to lose 2-0 to Wycombe. Mind you something should have been done about the tackle on Craig. Ainsworth should have seen red for that, which might have meant a different result as well. Oh well, that is what happens to us I suppose. It really was a bad injury. Fractured cheekbone and eye socket, and not even a yellow card for the perpetrator of this foot high tackle.

* * *

24 November 2009, Exeter City 1 – 1 Millwall
There was wind and rain in Exeter and that is what undid us in the 1-1 draw there. We should have scored more than just Martin's penalty and their goal was a fluke but all the same we should have won, especially as they only had ten men for a lot of the game.

Price is not good enough and although Morison hit a post I will be kind and say he is still learning the game at this level.

What about Grimes or Grabban?

Smith is injured now as well. Will we ever be injury free this season?

* * *

Well that is it then. The end of the final day for loan transfers and nobody in or out, does no one want to come here or did we not try hard enough? We will have to wait and see what happens in the January transfer window now.

Staines in the cup tomorrow and will Scott Taylor be the thorn in our side?

If Grimes was going to go on loan to Crawley but it got called off because of our injury problems, then he can't be in Jackett's plans for the future can he.

It is Friday and Danny Schofield is ill. All right it is not an injury but all the same!

* * *

28 November 2009, English FA Cup, Staines Town 1 – 1 Millwall
A 1-1 draw against Staines and Robinson's header was a bit lucky as well. Not sure about their penalty but again we made enough chances to win and we tried all the available strikers in Morison, Price, Grimes and Grabban. We need a striker and quickly. Still at least we are in the draw tomorrow.

* * *

It is Derby County in round three and they are beatable, but we need to get past Staines first and playing like we are, we won't beat either of them.

DECEMBER

1 December 2009, Millwall 3 – 2 Milton Keynes Dons
What a win against MK Dons. A 3-2 win sounds close and I guess it was, but the goals from Frampton, Hackett and Morison were all well taken. Can this be the start for Morison? I hope so, however, I would like to know how Easter stayed on the pitch. He did take both his goals well though. Why is it old players come back to bite you on the bum?

* * *

It is Friday and Dave Martin is injured. Say no more!

* * *

5 December 2009, Hartlepool United 3 – 0 Millwall
Morison hit the post and the bar at Hartlepool. Maybe he needs his luck changing. However, we lost 3-0 and this is the type of form that will take us out of the cup on Wednesday night.

* * *

9 December 2009, English FA Cup, Millwall 4 – 0 Staines Town
Well it did not and although we made hard work of it, Morison, Smith, Dunne and Schofield made the result look good in the end. We will need to play better against Walsall on Saturday to win that game and as I have said before, the game against Derby is winnable so let's get on with it.

David Forde is stalling on a new contract. He was going nowhere when we brought him in and made him the number one goalkeeper but I think he is a good goalkeeper and I hope he sorts things out, and signs soon.

That nice Mr Lacey is causing trouble again. Why doesn't he just sell his shares and be done with it. At least John Berylson has proved himself to be a good chairman, but now because Lacey won't allow a new share option we will have to borrow money again. I know it is from Berylson and his company but all the same we should not have to do that. Mind you the rest of football seems to be in financial trouble and some club will go to the wall soon.

* * *

12 December 2009, Millwall 2 – 1 Walsall
A good win at home against Walsall and we came from behind with both goals from Steve Morison. I hope that now shuts up the Morison's baiters for a while at least. We should have had two penalties for handball but I think we got away with one by Robinson so I will stop there, but another ref who missed things. Where do they get them from?

The newspapers are saying we are after Wayne Rooney's brother John. That is probably all it is, paper talk, but I suppose it is good for a laugh.

What a great idea to have the families of Jimmy Mizen and Rob Knox on the pitch before the Charlton game and all of them plus both teams wearing shirts with the slogan 'Anti Street Violence' on them. Well done also to both club's shirt sponsors for allowing it. Will the national press report it? It is doubtful.

It will be interesting to see Tony Craig in a mask if he plays on Saturday, if it allows him to play while the bones in his face are healing then why not.

* * *

19 December 2009, Charlton Athletic 4 – 4 Millwall
What a game against Charlton but the score does not do us justice. A 4-4 draw and a really exciting match, especially the way we came back. Great goals from Morison (2), Martin and Schofield; even if Morison's second was a tap in.

Yet again another poor referee. He gave Charlton two penalties, ignored two good appeals from us and sent off Jimmy Abdou, and Morison also scored an own goal. I can't wait to get them at our place in March.

I am glad the club are going to appeal against Jimmy Abdou's red card as the referee was wrong in the first place and he could never have seen what happened.

* * *

Well done the FA for rescinding Jimmy's red card. Did not help on the day mind but at least justice was done in the end.

* * *

26 December 2009, Norwich City 2 – 0 Millwall
Losing 2-0 at Norwich is not such a bad thing. They are a good side. Mind you we should have had a penalty before they scored and we missed a few chances as well, but it was always going to be a hard game to get anything from. We desperately need three points against Bristol Rovers on Monday now.

* * *

28 December 2009, Millwall 2 – 0 Bristol Rovers
We got the points but it could have been so different. We got away with the
first half when they hit the woodwork twice, but changing Price for Grabban
was the answer and Morison's goal plus an own goal from them sealed a good
2-0 win in the end.

Their own goal could not have happened to a nicer block, Pat Baldwin. He
should have seen red and had a penalty awarded against him so that is what I
call poetic justice.

JANUARY

Today sees the opening of the transfer window and we have signed Darren
Ward permanently until the end of the season. I am glad about that, as we
need as much experience at the back as we can get and he certainly has that.

Goodbye James Henry, again. Did not see much of him this time round due
to injury, but he certainly helped with some great goals and a few points. Will
we see him again? Who knows?

* * *

2 January 2010, English FA Cup, Millwall 1 – 1 Derby County
What is going on with our strike force? On the face of it a 1-1 draw with
Derby seems a good score and Grabban took his goal well but we missed a
hatful of chances again, and we totally outplayed them. If we go out of the
cup we only have ourselves to blame and we have got either Brentford or
Doncaster in the next round. That is a winnable game as well.

I heard we might be signing Liam Trotter on loan – again. Did not think
much of him last time round so I hope he is better this time.

* * *

Trotter signed for a month but I will reserve judgement until he goes. While
we are at it there is talk about us signing Lee Barnard. Now that would be a
good signing as he is a decent striker but I do not think he'll come here.

The snow has caused the cancellation of a lot of games at the weekend including
ours at Carlisle. I hope it turns out in our favour when we do play them.

It seems that Gary Alexander's season is over as the injury has not healed
properly and he might need surgery.

What is David Forde up to stalling on a new contract? If he is looking for
somewhere else then maybe the Hungarian we have on trial, Danny Illyes,
might be his replacement.

I am glad to hear that Peter Garston is doing well with his battle against
cancer. He has done a great job as the fan on the board and I would like to see

him do it for as long as he can and as long as he wants to. I'd certainly vote for him again.

I got a bit worried when I read that John Berylson was looking at offers for the club but it turned out that he was only looking at ways to improve things at the club and not thinking of selling to speculators. As far as I am concerned he is the best chairman we have had since Reg Burr. By the way, why are we still waiting to name a stand after him?

I am no fan of facebook but I can't believe fans have been thinking that they are talking to Alexander, Harris or Craig. Mind you, you have to be a bit stupid to impersonate them anyway as whoever it was would be sure to get found out.

* * *

Goodbye Zak. Hope you like Norwich. I for one will be sad to see you go as I thought you were a good player but it will be interesting to see what happens when the Canaries play us.

* * *

12 January 2010, English FA Cup, Derby County 1 – 1 Millwall (Derby won on penalties)
It was 1-1 again against Derby at their place and once more we should have had more to show for our efforts than Morison's goal. We hit the woodwork three times and I know they did the same to us twice but we must put these chances away.

Shame Schofield had his penalty saved but losing on penalties shows we can live at this level and now we need to show some consistency in front of goal and make a playoff place ours.

All charges have been dropped against us in the West Ham farce and so they should be, but why have West Ham only been fined £50,000? That is more than it cost us to defend ourselves and we won't get our money back. Hope we sue the FA for the money.

* * *

16 January 2010, Millwall 1 – 1 Southampton
How can my heart stand it? Two goals in the final minute and we get a 1-1 draw with Southampton. I must hand it to the team and to Trotter for getting the goal. They never thought it was a lost cause.

We are still getting rubbish referees though. Maybe that is the way the FA will get their own back after the West Ham thing and to think we were presented with the Racial Equality Standard before the game as well. We are the first club to get it so what do you say about that my media friends? Nothing as usual when something good is happening.

We are supposed to be after Theo Robinson from Huddersfield, and we need another striker now that Alexander has had his operation and will be out for the rest of the season.

I have just read that Kenny Jackett says he has no idea where the Robinson story came from. Oh well!

* * *

23 January 2010, Oldham Athletic 0 – 1 Millwall

Harris' penalty was enough to win the game at Oldham and it was good to see the referee and his assistant on our side for a change. We could have done without him getting injured though but things are starting to look up for us.

Well we have got our striker in Shaun Batt, who signed on loan until the end of the season from Peterborough, and with Harris injured he will probably play tomorrow.

* * *

26 January 2010, Millwall 2 – 0 Southend United

Batt did play and scored one of the goals in our 2-0 win over Southend, Schofield scored the other one. He did not have bad debut. He is quick and took his goal well and he puts himself about a bit, although his first touch needs working on.

It was a scrappy game though and we are back to dodgy referees. I knew having good ones would not last long.

As it is the club's 125th year next season we are having a special dark blue shirt, and the fans have been asked to vote on whether the numbers and collars are white or gold. I like the gold one myself so I will vote for that.

Robinson (three years), Forde (three years) and Harris (two years) have all signed new contracts and I for one am pleased about all three. Now let's make it worthwhile. Mind you it is another Friday and another injury, this time it is Danny Schofield. What goes on in Bromley on a Friday?

* * *

30 January 2010, Brighton and Hove Albion 0 – 1 Millwall

A win at Brighton is always good and Morison's goal was enough to do it for us. Keep on winning boys and make that playoff spot ours.

FEBRUARY

The transfer window closed last night and we did a bit of business. Jason Price went to Oldham on loan for a month and Marcus Bignot had his contract cancelled. I am not too displeased with Price as he was not really doing it for us but it is a shame about Bignot, although he never had a chance of getting into the side since his injury, and with the team playing like it is.

We have also signed Trotter on loan until the end of the season and I must say I have been pleasantly surprised with him. He's put on a bit of muscle and grown up a lot since he was here last and he's doing a good job for us in the middle of the park, even though a lot of fans do not seem to appreciate what he does.

Dave Martin could have gone to Derby for £200,000 but he could not agree personal terms. Another greedy player who thinks he is better than he is. He would not have been a great loss as far as I am concerned as he has lost his way a bit this season.

Oh no! Kenny Jackett is up for the manager of the month award again. I know we beat the curse last time but can we do it twice if he wins it?

* * *

Hackett and Dunne have both been offered new contracts and I hope they sign as both of them have had good seasons and deserve it, and Danny Senda has played sixty-five minutes in a reserve game. Now that could prove interesting.

* * *

6 February 2010, Millwall 2 – 1 Norwich City

We beat Norwich 2-1 with goals from Craig and Harris after being a goal down, but it should have been three as the referee cheated us out of a goal.

Whitbread came on as a substitute and pulled Morison down in the box. He should have been sent off as he was the last man and we should have had a penalty but the referee bottled it – again. There was not a single booking in the match. Is that some sort of record?

The loan window has opened and Martin has gone to Derby until the end of the season when he will be a free agent. We will get nothing for him then but what if nobody wants him then. It would serve him right if it happens, the money grabber.

We have taken Jon Obika, a striker, on loan from Spurs until the end of the season. He is only nineteen but will be a good replacement for Price, I hope. Sadly we have cancelled Danny Senda's contract. I hope things work out for him.

* * *

Yes it is Friday and once more the dreaded Friday bug has struck again and this time twice. Schofield has cut his shin and Smith pulled a hamstring. I hate Fridays.

* * *

13 February 2010, Millwall 1 – 0 Exeter City

Obika made a short debut in the match against Exeter, who had a player, Barry Corr, sent off, but their goal had a charmed life and their goalkeeper made some exceptional saves. So it needed an exceptional free kick from Harris to win the match. Keep it up Bomber!

I have just read that we turned down the chance of taking Dean Cox on loan from Brighton and took Jon Obika instead. I do not understand why as I think Cox would have been a good addition to the squad and I do not know anything about Obika. Mind you I think Kenny Jackett knows what he is doing and gets more right than wrong, so time will tell.

* * *

20 February 2010, Wycombe Wanderers 1 – 0 Millwall

A freak goal and a penalty miss by Harris and we lose 1-0 at Wycombe, and to add to that, Dunne hit the bar. Mind you it was only justice that Ainsworth got sent off for putting his elbow in Craig's face, as he should have walked in the game at The Den, and he was only on the pitch for about five minutes. What does he have against Craig?

We need to get back on track at MK Dons on Tuesday or promotion will slip quietly away, and so might the playoffs.

* * *

23 February 2010, Milton Keynes Dons 1 – 3 Millwall

We got back on track all right. A goal from Schofield and two from Harris gets the confidence back straight away. Shame we let one in.

We could, and probably should, have scored more and although we are still out of the top six, the gap is closing up again, although we are starting to pull away from eighth spot now. It is all to play for.

Why did I think that we would not get charged by the FA for the fight at Wycombe? How could they think there would be no trouble when Ainsworth did what he did again to Craig? Still I suppose that they had to do something to us, after what happened at the Hamsters place.

At last we have spent some money on the pitch, £3,000 to be exact. Let's hope it stops it from cutting up like it has been. So now let's play on it and not in the air.

Chris Hackett is going to sign a new two-and-a-half-year deal. I know he is not everybody's cup of tea, (mind you that goes for every player here at some time,) but I for one am glad.

* * *

27 February 2010, Millwall 1 – 0 Hartlepool United
It is the fourth Dockers Day today and this has become a great tradition. Hope we keep it going for as long as possible. However, it seems that all the money spent on the pitch was a waste of time, unless it settles down soon. It spoilt the match really and made Hartlepool look better than I think they are but it was about time we won a game with a fluke goal. Well done Neil Harris.

MARCH

John Sullivan has been offered a new one-year deal. I can't really comment on him as we have only seen him once. However, every side needs a decent back up goalkeeper and Jackett must think he is that to offer him the contract so I hope he signs.

With Jackett up for his second manager of the month award and Harris nominated for player of the month, the old gremlins could have a field day. Mind you we beat it last time so why not again? Having said that, let's not win it and we do not have to worry.

I was sad to see Adam Bolder going on loan to Bradford, but it will do him good and he was never going to get back into the side unless things went dramatically wrong. It will help him when the end of the season comes as I think he will be one of a few to go.

I am getting a bit concerned about the crowd at the Charlton game next week. It is a sell out and all the usual troublemakers coming out of the woodwork, with all eyes on us. I really hope I am wrong.

At least Sam Parkin won't be playing for Walsall at the weekend but that still leaves 'Baby Boy' and Vincent, although we coped with them at our place.

* * *

6 March 2010, Walsall 2 – 2 Millwall
Well we are back in a playoff spot (sixth) now, Swindon and Huddersfield losing helped. At least we have proved to ourselves that we can be a force to be reckoned with.

Two goals down and Morison and Dunne salvage a point. Dunne's late equaliser would be a contender for goal of the season as well. Shame Craig only hit the bar but I suppose I should not be greedy. Yes I should. They were down to ten men for half an hour when Marc Richard was sent off for the umpteenth foul on Hackett.

Good job Jackett did not win the manager of the month award or we would have lost this one but as Harris won the player of the month maybe that is why he did not play.

* * *

9 March 2010, Carlisle United 1 – 3 Millwall

Two goals from Morison and another from Schofield gave us a good 1-3 win at Carlisle, and with Swindon losing again we have now grabbed fifth place. Two massive games next against Charlton and Leeds to come, I just hope we can get something from them.

It must have been an interesting night at Carlisle last night as Jason Price stayed there on loan until the end of the season. I do not really expect him to come back to The Den next season anyway as he is not good enough.

I must say I agree with the club about the fans behaviour at the Charlton game. The world and his dog will be watching us and there is bound to be a few interlopers looking to cause problems, and of course a few mixed fans. So please for all of our sakes everyone behave.

What a shame Gary Alexander did not win the goal of the year with his Wembley goal. I thought it was the best one but then again I am probably biased. To be fair Nicky Maynard's was a very good goal.

* * *

13 March 2010, Millwall 4 – 0 Charlton Athletic

Why did I worry about the fans at this game? Mind you the score might have had something to do with it. Two from Morison, one from Ward and a lovely own goal from Dailly (he must love coming here), and Charlton rarely bothered us.

Now we are in fourth and good business by Jackett loaning Price to Carlisle as he scored the winner against Colchester that helped move us up. Yippee. Now we need to go after an automatic spot. Bring on Leeds.

* * *

There are not many fans going to Elland Road and I can't say that I blame them with all the problems we have getting into their ground. The best way to get our own back is to beat them.

Sullivan signed that new contract and (I can't believe I am saying this) I am glad that Dunne has signed a new one as well. He has certainly come on well in the second half of this season and I can only congratulate him for the way he has changed himself around both in his attitude and his playing. Well done Dunney, now keep it up.

I am not happy about the club moving the Brentford match from the Saturday to Good Friday. I understand why they did it with Colchester doing the same with their game. I just hope it proves to be worth it.

* * *

22 March 2010, Leeds United 0 – 2 Millwall

Well done those 375 fans that made the trip to Elland Road. You deserve to have seen a great 0-2 win. Well done Morison and Batt for the goals and well done everyone for a great game. Forde did not have a shot to save.

It was good to see Bolder, Grabban, Alexander and Tony Warner in with the fans. It shows a great team spirit. Up to third now and only three points behind Leeds, and they play Norwich on Saturday. We must not mess it up against Stockport on Saturday.

It makes sense to me to let Marquis and Hughes-Mason go out on loan so that they can get more experience, and Grabban going to Brentford probably means he will be on his way at the end of the season. It is interesting about Grimes though, he is still here. Did nobody want him or is Jackett keeping him, only time will tell.

* * *

27 March 2010, Millwall 5 – 0 Stockport County

Five goals against Stockport sounds great and to be honest it was, so what if two of them were own goals. We still had to create them and the goals from Morison, Schofield and Obika were well worth it. Harris hit the bar and we could have had a lot more, and with Leeds losing at Norwich it is down to goal difference now. Mind you it is very close as any one of five clubs can still snatch second place. Norwich has the top spot sewn up now.

I was pleased to read that Jackett says that Laird and Fuseini can still get new contracts for next season. If they go we will still need to bring others in although if we get Trotter that is something. But we will have to replace Bolder as well. Can we really allow ourselves to be three and possibly four midfield players short at the end of the season?

APRIL

It is good to know our finances are getting better. All right we still made a loss of £2.5 million but that is a bit better than this time last year.

At least the crowds are getting bigger and we need to keep that happening until the end of the season. However, I am sure that will happen as the team are playing well and all the glory hunting fans will make an appearance as we get closer to the season's end and We have a chance of going up automatically.

I just wish we could see a bit more of them through the rest of the season as it would make things a lot better from a financial point of view.

With Jackett nominated once more for the manager of the month and Morison the player of the month I am glad we play Brentford on Friday night before the winners are announced. The problem then will be the game at Colchester on Monday. Oh well!

* * *

2 April 2010, Millwall 1 – 1 Brentford

A 1-1 draw against Brentford and that old, score five in the game before syndrome, raises its ugly head again. I did not think we would score all night even after Harris hit the post so I am glad Robinson stuck it away.

Mind you, their goal was well offside and the referee and his assistant made some very dodgy decisions all night. We've been having some fairly good referees lately so I suppose it was only a matter of time before things got back to normal.

Anyway we are second now, even if it is just for the night, so let's enjoy it, see what happens on Saturday and get a win at Colchester on Monday.

* * *

Oh no. Jackett won the manager of the month and Morison player of the month. Hope our season does not end here.

What a strange Saturday. Swindon beat Leeds so they go second, we are third and Leeds fourth. Norwich lose at Tranmere but stay on top, Charlton win at MK Dons and move into fifth, Colchester drop to seventh after losing to Exeter with Huddersfield moving into sixth after beating Wycombe.

They are the side to watch out for I think, as there is always one team that come good right at the death. What an interesting Monday we have in store now.

* * *

5 April 2010, Colchester United 1 – 2 Millwall

Thank you Mr own goal, add another goal from Morison and we moved into second, if only for a little while. We should have had more though as we had two stonewall penalties turned down by that nice Andy D'urso.

Mind you it was poor defending on our part for Colchester's goal and we need to be careful about letting those in as I can see goal difference playing a part in who finishes where, especially as Swindon and Leeds both won again as well.

That last game of the season seems to be taking on more importance as time goes by, especially if they stay in second with us third as it is now.

I am glad to hear that Tony Craig has been given a new two-year contract. I love his enthusiasm and I love the way he plays. Keeping a consistent squad will do us a lot of good next season no matter what happens. Now go and offer a new contract to Darren Ward.

* * *

It is Friday and that means another injury and this time it is Alan Dunne. Good job we have an able replacement for him in Jack Smith. I wonder if the tables have been turned for these two again.

* * *

10 April 2010, Millwall 4 – 0 Gillingham

A great 4-0 win against the 'Gills' and the goals from Batt, Craig, Schofield and Harris were all brilliant.

In fact Craig's will be another contender for goal of the season if television could be bothered to look outside the Premier League. If one of those precious players scored a goal like that we would be watching it for months to come.

So we are back in second place with Swindon losing and it is a shame that Leeds won as that would have opened a nice gap, so we need to do it again on Tuesday against Yeovil.

At least we have got passed the ten booking, two match ban mark, so Morison and Batt can rest easier now for the rest of the season.

* * *

13 April 2010, Yeovil Town 1 – 1 Millwall

How can we be so good and then so bad three days later? Obika's last gasp effort gave us a draw, which is a point that might make all the difference come the day of reckoning.

Mind you it is a strange season. Leeds have gone back into second place, we have dropped to third and now Southampton look like they might grab a place in the top six as well. We really do need to beat Huddersfield on Friday night now or I can see it all going wrong and we will slip out of the top six all together.

It is interesting news that we are pulling out of the reserve league for next season and playing friendly matches. There were not many games this season and players coming into the team look rusty for a while. Keeping them match fit, even if it is at a lower level, will be important.

Make sure Richard Shaw is kept on as well as he is an important part of the coaching setup.

* * *

16 April 2010, Huddersfield Town 1 – 0 Millwall

I really hate Fridays and losing to Huddersfield proves it. The goal was a bad mistake by Forde, again, but we did not play well.

Losing Batt so early in the match did not help, and with Trotter and Dunne both out injured and a half fit Hackett, we really struggled but it was good to see Alexander on the pitch if only for a very short time.

Things might have been different if Obika's effort had gone in instead of hitting the bar but you can't live on what might have been. At least we only need one more point to guarantee a play-off place and unless a miracle happens that is all we can look forward to now.

* * *

Miracles happen. Leeds and Charlton lost and Swindon drew so it is game on again, although Norwich have now taken one of the promotion spots and I have no doubt will go up as champions.

We will still need to win our last three games and Leeds to drop points, and now goal difference becomes a real factor. If only Forde had caught that ball on Friday night.

No surprises in being fined £2,500 for the fight at Wycombe. Still it could have been worse so let's pay the fine and run.

* * *

No, no, no. Just as you thought it couldn't get worse it does. Tony Craig has injured his ankle and looks like he could be out for the rest of the season. Here we go again.

Things must be bad as we have recalled Louis Grabban from Brentford. I know he has been doing well there but I have never really been sure about him. He has something there but often never seems to produce it.

* * *

Craig's injury does not seem to be as bad as first thought so he might get to play again which will boost the squad as well.

Are we starting to see the departure of Graham Lacey? Now he has decided to sell some of his shares he might have begun to get a bit bored with us and sell a few more. I hope so.

Thank you CYC for putting your money into the club for another three years. It is the sort of stability we need and like John Berylson sticking with us, will do the club the world of good.

* * *

24 April 2010, Millwall 2 – 1 Leyton Orient

Well it looked a bit of a struggle against Orient at times but a win is a win and after Robinson's goal settled the nerves, Morison's penalty settled the game. Well done Neil Harris for giving the ball to him so that he could reach the twenty goal mark.

We should not have let in their late goal though as we have now lost out on the goal difference tally, and still being third that could now make all the difference.

Come on Charlton and Bristol Rovers. I never thought I would hear myself say that.

Congratulations Zampa on your London Marathon run. Five hours and fifteen minutes is no mean feat in those conditions and well done for all the money you raised for the Everyman Appeal. In fact, well done all Millwall fans for your donations or your efforts in raising money for whatever charity it was.

I am not surprised that Morison won the Junior Lions player of the year and he will probably get the main one as well. Personally I would like to see Schofield get it, but a player scoring goals like Morison has been doing, always seems to win the most votes.

I have just read that Ipswich are letting Trotter go on a free in the summer. Come on Kenny, act now and get his signature.

MAY

1 May 2010, Tranmere Rovers 2 – 0 Millwall

This promotion lark is not good for the old ticker. We lose 2-0 at Tranmere, Charlton beat Leeds (thank you), and Swindon and Huddersfield both win, so now any one of the five of us could get the second spot on Saturday.

We just need to beat Swindon and Leeds not win, and it is ours. Not asking for much am I?

There will be a lot of frayed nerves around on Saturday both on the pitch and in the stands at all the clubs involved.

Well the future of the club looks good on the playing front as the under eighteens won their league. Let's hope a couple of the players there make it into the first team as Marquis and Hughes-Mason have already done this season.

* * *

What a surprise, Alan Dunne winning the player of the year award. I must say that he has turned around both his attitude and his playing in the second half of the season, so well done Dunney. Now keep it up.

Well this is it, squeaky bum time and things are not looking good. Morison has a late fitness test, Schofield and Dunne are definitely out, Craig and Batt probably are out and we still need Leeds not to win. All I can say is – JUST BELIEVE.

* * *

8 May 2010, Millwall 3 – 2 Swindon Town

Well we won the game but not the spot, although at one point we did hold the second place. Another own goal and two from Morison, one a penalty, gave us the win we wanted and we had to come from behind after Swindon took the lead, and then held on after they pulled it back to 3-2. But Leeds managed to grab a 2-1 win and pinched second place from us by a point.

Mind you, one good thing came out of the last day of the season results – Gillingham were relegated again.

Yes we could go through all the 'what ifs' etc., but it won't change anything. So it is two matches against Huddersfield and then hopefully another trip to Wembley. At least the queue at The Den for tickets was not too bad. So it is off to the Galpharm Stadium for a 12.15 p.m. kick off on Saturday. Then we will see what we need to do the following Tuesday night for a game against either Charlton or Swindon at Wembley.

Will it be sixth time lucky in the playoffs or third time lucky for a win at Wembley? Here we go again and only time will tell.

* * *

Hackett is out injured now so adding him to Dunne, Batt and Schofield it will be difficult getting passed Huddersfield now. We will just have to get on with it though and see what happens.

* * *

15 May 2010, League One Play-Off First Leg, Huddersfield Town 0 – 0 Millwall

I am not sure a 0-0 draw is as good a result as it seems. Yes it was a good result for us given the circumstances especially as we should have had two nailed on penalties but there you go. This is Millwall we are talking about. There is no doubt that had they been the other way around they would have been given.

The policing was poor as well and I hope that everyone sees the YouTube film of the two policemen punching that young fan. If West Yorkshire police do not do something about that then we might as well all give up now.

* * *

18 May 2010, League One Play-Off Second Leg, Millwall 2 – 0 Huddersfield Town

We are going to Wembley. Great to see Schofield back in the side and what a set up for an easy goal for Morison, and Robbo's goal was the icing on the cake. He deserves to get us there after the disappointment of last year.

Shame that Barron's shot hit the bar. That was worthy of winning the match on its own, still must not be greedy. It was an easy win really as we dominated the game so bring on Swindon.

What a shame about the fools that ran onto the pitch as it would have been good to see the players take a bow. I know they were only enjoying themselves and it should have been expected of course but it spoilt the night a bit.

I cannot wait for Friday to get my Wembley ticket.

* * *

Here we go again. We have been given the east end of the stadium, just like last year. Hope the final result is different though.

I wish Morison would stop talking about being at Wembley for the third time and never having lost before. Maybe I am overreacting but I am a Millwall fan and we all know what that means.

The ticket office was its usual problem and why were the good seats all put onto the online sales with nobody being told? What a waste of queuing all night. Somebody needs to sort this out if we ever have to do it again.

It is a shame that Fuseini has been told he can go but he has not really come on over the last season but I am pleased that Laird has been offered a contract. He does more than a lot of fans give him credit for. Now offer Ward one as well.

I am getting worried about the Wembley pitch. The players in the Championship playoff were moaning about it and so were the England players after the Mexico game. What will it be like when we play on it? Hope it is not the reason for something going wrong.

Looks like Ward might be offered a contract for next season. It has been good having him back. Apart from a short spell early on, he has played well.

I must admit I was wrong about Trotter and now he has been put on Ipswich's release list I hope we get him as well. Mind you now we have shown an interest, they have offered him a contract which means we will have to pay something for him because of his age. Don't shirk it Kenny, go and get him.

Talk of Steve Morison being a Welsh international sounds good. It will put a few extra zeros on his transfer value but worse than that it will make even more clubs aware of what he can do and they will be after him. Will we keep him then if the offer is even a moderately good one? I will be pleased for him though if he makes it that far. He has had a good season for us so I hope he does the business again in the next one, whatever division we are in.

* * *

Well done Millwall for giving the mascot place at Wembley to George Mizzen. Will the papers pick it up? Of course not, good things and Millwall are still not worthy of a news report.

I have just read that John Berylson says that it is promotion, not the money, which he is after. It is the right thing to say of course and if he means it good on him but let's face it the cash won't go amiss.

* * *

Are the bookies kidding? We have been made 28-1 to win promotion to the Premier League next season. We have not even made it out of League One yet. Still I suppose it shows what they think about the game on Saturday and I hope they are right.

Right: Winning goal-scorer and captain, Paul Robinson, holds the play-off trophy aloft, while Chairman John Berylson (far right) applauds. (*Brian Tonks*)

Below: Paul Robinson kissing the cup. (*Brian Tonks*)

The players celebrate after winning promotion to the Championship at Wembley. (*Brian Tonks*)

Goal-scorer Paul Robinson celebrates with the play-off trophy. (*Brian Tonks*)

* * *

It is Friday and yes we have another injury. This time it is Jack Smith. He must be gutted, missing out from playing at Wembley, especially against his old club. But what do we do now as Dunne is out as well. If Hackett is fit maybe he will play at right back, but if not then who else will play there?

Mind you I hope Barron does not miss out as he has been great over the last few weeks and deserves a place in the team.

Am I nervous? No. Am I a liar? Yes. Just look at the number of times I cut myself shaving this morning. Mind you it is a strange feeling. Not really nerves but something that says this is it.

* * *

29 May 2010, League One Play-Off Final, Millwall 1 – 0 Swindon Town

An easy win in the end and well done Robbo for scoring what turned out to be the only goal of the game, although I suppose we have the now infamous Wembley turf to thank for that and especially for Austin's miss right at the end. I think Morison looked a bit out of sorts but to be fair the whole team did a workmanlike job and they got what they deserved. What a way for Super Neil Harris to play his 400th match.

Championship here we come.

INDEX